ISO 27001:2022

Information Security Management System Guide

Bruce Brown, CISSP, CGRC

Sources and downloadable:

The main authoritative resource for ISO 27001 is
https://www.iso.org/

You can also check out my downloadables at
http://convocourses.com/courses/iso27000

Check us out on:

youtube.com/@convocourses

Contact us:

contact@convocourses.com

Contents

An International Security Standard

Question: "What Do You Do When One Size Does NOT fit ALL?"

Different systems and information types have different business requirements and, therefore, different security.

When I was working as a cybersecurity risk consultant, we would determine the security risks of a company based on data from scans. We would run vulnerability, wireless, and other scans and then determine the highest risk levels. Another service we provided was to figure out what security controls they needed to apply more effectively. What I saw is that organizations that applied a set of security controls were the best prepared against attacks, mishaps, and other security incidents.

According to a Duke University/CFO Magazine Global Business Outlook study, over 80% of U.S. companies reported that their systems had been successfully hacked to steal, change, or make sensitive data public. The study includes firms from Asia, Europe, Africa, and Latin America.

Protecting systems is not merely about hiring talented people to guard against cyber attacks or implementing the latest technical solutions; it's also about implementing sound security processes. These processes come from frameworks and standards that guide an organization in the right direction. The right standard and framework are based on the needs of the organization.

Within different industries and sectors, you have distinct standards and laws, such as the healthcare Health Insurance Portability and Accountability Act (HIPAA), the US federal government's NIST 800 framework, or Payment Card Industry Data Security Standard (PCI-DSS) that the retail, hotel, and restaurant industries rely on. You have the financial industry's Sarbanes-Oxley Act(SOX), which has IT controls. There are dozens of other industries and sectors with sets of laws and controls they must abide by, but you also have nation-states with their own security needs.

Many countries have laws and standards that mandate the protection of systems that manage the sensitive data of their citizens.

But what if you have an organization that operates internationally? What if your organization has information systems that must be protected in the US, Canada, and parts of Europe or Asia? As a cybersecurity risk consultant, I saw global organizations with this challenge.

That's where the ISO 27001 comes in. ISO 27001 is created and maintained by an international body and is the most recognized, respected, and accepted international standard globally.

International Standards

Its official name is ISO/IEC 27001:2022, Information Security, Cybersecurity and Privacy Protection — Information Security Management Systems. This security standard uses "ISO" and "IEC" in the name because it was created and published by both the International Organization for Standardization (also known as "ISO") and the International Electrotechnical Commission (IEC).

These international organizations are composed of over 160 participating countries. Information system security is only a tiny sliver of what ISO does. They have published standards and rules in many technical and nontechnical areas.

If you've ever had to find a screw with exact threading, get a device to plug into a wall in another country or recycle an item, then you should appreciate that all of this is because of the agreed-upon national and international standards that allow us to take these conveniences for granted.

For example, ISO 9000 addresses quality management systems. ISO 14000 is for environmental management systems. ISO 2 covers the direction of twist designation for materials such as cordage and yarn. ISO 62 covers the water absorption of plastics. The highlighted ISO 27000 series is the Information system security, the best practice recommendations for managing information risks through information controls. Many other series and sets of ISO documents cover everything from human resources to electronic engineering.

What is IEC 27000?

The ISO/IEC 27000-series covers information security management systems (ISMS). It is sometimes called the 'ISMS Family of Standards' or 'ISO27K'. The ISMS provides best security practices in information security management.

The ISO 27000 series is broad and vendor-neutral to cover more information technology aspects, including privacy, technical issues, and cybersecurity. Since organizations come in all shapes and sizes and have many needs, 27000 has to be all-encompassing. Information risk and security are dynamic, so 27001's concept includes continuous feedback and improvement activities to respond to new threats, vulnerabilities, and impacts of incidents.

ISO/IEC 27001:2022 focuses on information security standards. It provides an organization's information security management system (ISMS) with formal guidelines on planning, implementing, and managing security. This standard is designed so that organizations can meet legal and regulatory requirements while optimally protecting their information assets. The standard is designed to require collaboration among all departments in the organization. The standard also clearly defines details for documentation, management responsibility, internal and external audits, and corrective and preventive action.

Why is ISO 27001 Important?

Cybercrime has become rampant nowadays. It targets all industries and all types of organizations. Even the focus of this type of crime has widened, from stealing personal data to crippling critical systems—everything is fair game. This is creating a hindrance for organizations to continue their normal systems functioning safely. The need of the hour is for security to be woven into systems and functioning instead of being added as an afterthought.

Often, many organizations lack the necessary capabilities to develop such an intricate security system independently. ISO 27001 has everything they need. It provides a comprehensive set of guidelines for determining what security controls should be implemented and how they should be implemented.

It starts with a big-picture view of security design and then drills down into the details of the individual protections that need to be implemented. It focuses on risk assessment activities to proactively identify and address security weaknesses. It promotes a holistic approach to information security, vetting people, policies, and technology. ISO 27001, with its requirement of periodic re-evaluations after implementation, can also help ensure that you remain compliant with industry regulations and meet the necessary standards. The standard also undergoes periodic revisions and adapts to evolving threats by amending the standard to include new threat vectors and attack surfaces. Being an industry standard, achieving and maintaining a third-party certification of ISO 27001 also helps you remain on par with the competition and provides you with an edge in your industry.

Benefits of ISO 27001

ISO 27001 provides organizations with a template for implementing security controls. It establishes a minimum standard of requirements to meet and provides guidelines for how to meet them. Implementing an ISMS according to ISO 27001:2022 can help organizations achieve resilience to cyberattacks, preparedness for new threats, data integrity, confidentiality, availability, security across all supports, organization-wide protection, and cost savings. Because of how it is designed, the standard can be applied to organizations of all sizes and across different industries. Let us look at some of the benefits of adopting ISO 27001:

- **Cybersecurity.** The biggest and possibly the most obvious benefit of implementing ISO 27001 is for an organization to avoid the cost of a potential security breach. While you may argue that implementing the standard will also require investment, the cost of a data breach or attack could be much higher.

- **Reputation.** The reputational damage from a security breach can be significant and take years, if not decades, to recover. Implementing ISO 27001 protects your reputation, and getting your organization certified can also enhance it, making you an industry leader, lending you credibility, and encouraging people and other businesses to work with you.

- **Compliance.** ISO 27001 is a framework that guides the selection of appropriate and proportional security controls to protect information assets. This standard is particularly relevant under stringent regulatory requirements such as the General Data Protection Regulation (GDPR) and the Network and Information Systems (NIS) Directive. While ISO 27001 is not a direct compliance requirement for

GDPR or NIS, implementing its best practices can significantly aid in meeting obligations. By aligning with ISO 27001, organizations can enhance compliance with these regulations and reduce the risk of legal repercussions. Moreover, ISO 27001 offers a robust approach to securing valuable information assets, providing high security.

- **Standard.** ISO 27001 provides a framework for implementing the most effective security controls tailored to your organization's and industry's specific needs. This standard is crucial in protecting sensitive customer information, critical infrastructure, and intellectual property. Additionally, ISO 27001's comprehensive approach to information security management can be instrumental in securely adopting emerging technologies such as Artificial Intelligence (AI) and cloud computing. It helps ensure that these technologies are integrated into your organization's environment in a way that maintains data integrity, confidentiality, and availability.

- **Organizational Structure.** It can help to improve the organizational structure. With rapid growth, the company often has disorganization as the lines of roles and responsibilities blur. Implementing ISO 27001 can help define this structure clearly and help organizations become more productive by clearly setting out information risk responsibilities. Having this clarity can provide benefits such as:

  - Increased productivity: When there is clarity on who is responsible for which information assets, productivity is automatically improved, and there is no duplication of effort.

- Improved decision-making: Organizations can better manage information risks by understanding the risks involved.

- Reduced costs: a clear and concise structure for managing information risks can help organizations recognize the proper capital distribution and avoid wasted efforts.

⬡ **Certification.** ISO 27001 certification can reduce the need for customer audits and frequent external audits, as it indicates security effectiveness. Because ISO certification requires regular reviews and internal audits, it ensures your security posture is up to date and is the most effective plan for your organization.

Chapter 1

Understanding ISO 27001

There is a quote from the movie Age of Ultron where Tony Stark (aka Iron Man) says, "I see a suit of armor around the world.

It's a metaphor for a singular security solution powerful enough to protect the Earth and all humans from a hostile alien threat.

<u>Let's be clear: ISO 27001 is absolutely NOT what Iron Man was talking about</u>. In fact, it's fair to say ISO 27001 has nothing to do with the Marvel Cinematic Universe.

But it **is** an international standard for protecting computers and computer data that is used all over the world! ISO 27001 will probably not stop an "Avenger" level threat like Thanos. However, it **is** used at The Walt Disney Company to protect its multi-billion-dollar intellectual property (property like the Marvel Cinematic Universe data files). Would it be a stretch to say that ISO 27001 is protecting Thanos from being "snapped" out of existence by a would-be criminal hacker?

The official name of ISO 27001 is ISO/IEC 27001:2022, Information Security, Cybersecurity and Privacy Protection — Information Security Management Systems.

The term "Information Security Management System" or ISMS is important if you want to understand ISO 27001.

We will use the term "ISMS" throughout this book. It's important to understand that an organization's information security management system is not just a bunch of documentation. Yes, the policies and procedures are an important part of the ISMS. Still, these documents are just tools for managing a system that creates and maintains the organization's security.

ISMS consists of three major components: people, processes, and technology. These three components form the pillars of a good ISMS: the fuel, machinery, and spark that keeps the ISMS working. People are arguably the most important aspect of an ISMS, as they are the ones who plan for, design, document, implement, and maintain an ISMS. Processes and technology must be chosen carefully and updated regularly to remove any loopholes that changing technology may introduce. Proper management of these three components is critical for maintaining the organization's confidentiality, integrity, and availability of information.

- **Confidentiality** – Confidentiality refers to protecting sensitive information from unauthorized access and disclosure. Issues in managing confidentiality often stem from inadequate access controls, insufficient data encryption, and a lack of awareness among employees about the importance of safeguarding sensitive information. ISO/IEC 27001 emphasizes the need for a comprehensive ISMS that includes robust access control measures to manage information access and prevent unauthorized data sharing, intentionally or accidentally.

- **Integrity** – Integrity means maintaining the original meaning and intent of the information. Consider a scenario where your company shares information about its senior managers online. The accuracy of this information is paramount for maintaining integrity. Inaccurate details could erode trust, giving the impression of unreliability to those seeking information on your website. Furthermore, there is a potential threat where malicious attackers try to compromise the website's security, altering executive descriptions, photographs, or titles to impact the company's reputation detrimentally. This underscores the necessity of ensuring the precision and security of information to safeguard the overall trustworthiness of the organization.

- **Availability** – Availability is the ability to access the information, system or service. To secure continuous availability, organizations can implement redundant networks, servers, and applications designed to activate in the event of disruptions or failures in the primary system. Proactively managing software package upgrades and security system enhancements further contributes to heightened availability by reducing the risks of application malfunctions or vulnerabilities to emerging threats.

Additionally, establishing robust backup systems and comprehensive disaster recovery plans is pivotal in swiftly restoring availability in the aftermath of adverse events.

The ISO 27000 series is designed to guide an organization through the information security management systems process. Some of the most essential ISO 27000 standards include:

- ISO/IEC 27001:2022 - defines the framework for ISMS.
- ISO/IEC 27002:2022 – Guide for implementing security controls.
- ISO/IEC 27005:2022 – Guide for risk management of the ISMS.

ISO/IEC 27001:2022 provides a big-picture approach to an organization's security process. 27001 is broken into the following clauses:

Context of the Organization (Clause 4): Involves understanding internal and external factors and needs of interested parties, defining the scope, and establishing the ISMS.

Leadership (Clause 5): Focuses on top management's roles in leading and supporting the ISMS.

Planning (Clause 6): Involves addressing risks and opportunities and setting information security objectives.

Support (Clause 7): Covers resources, competence, awareness, communication, and managing documented information.

Operation (Clause 8): Discusses planning, risk assessment, and risk treatment.

Performance Evaluation (Clause 9): Involves monitoring, internal audit, and management review.

Improvement (Clause 10): Addresses nonconformities and corrective actions for continual improvement.

Each clause is integral to the framework of the ISMS and contributes to the overall effectiveness and compliance of an organization's information security management.

Clauses 4 – 10 are the ones that the organization must implement to get an ISO 27001 certification.

The ISO 27000 series adapts the Plan-Do-Check-Act (PDCA) method to develop, implement, and continuously improve the information security management system. We will address how the clauses and the PDCA merge to complete the ISMS process, but first, let's address the PDCA.

Plan-Do-Check-Act (PDCA)

The Plan-Do-Check-Act (PDCA) model is integral to the ISO 27001 information security management system standard.

It outlines requirements for establishing, implementing, maintaining, and continually improving an Information Security Management System within the organization's context.

The PDCA cycle in ISO/IEC 27001 is typically described as follows:

1. **Plan:** Establish the ISMS by defining policies, objectives, processes, and procedures relevant to managing risk and improving information security to deliver results in accordance with an organization's overall policies and objectives.

2. **Do:** Implement and operate the ISMS by executing the planned processes and procedures.

3. **Check:** Monitor and review the performance of the ISMS against the policies, objectives, and practical experiences and report the results to management for review.

4. **Act:** Take corrective and preventive actions, based on the results of the management review, to continually improve the performance of the ISMS.

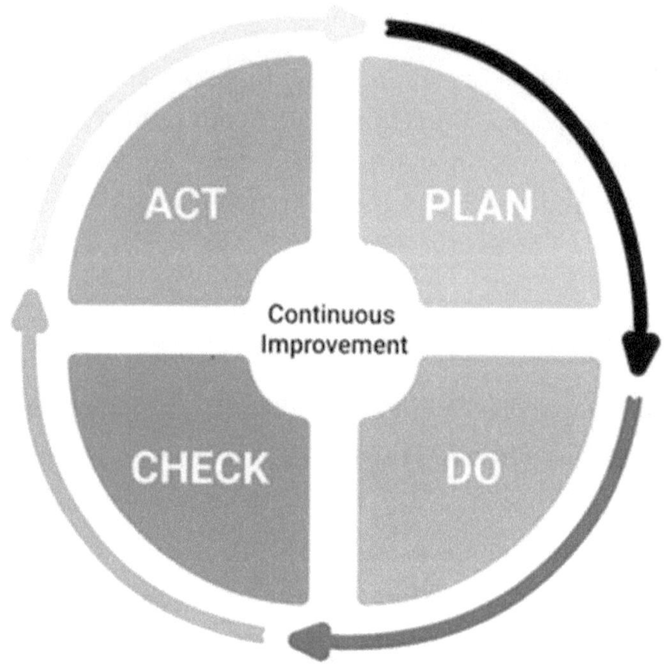

The PDCA process implements ISO 27001 "clauses." If you can grasp the Plan-Do-Check-Act and how it connects to each ISO 27001 clause, you are on your way to mastering this respected international ISMS.

7 Clauses of ISO 27001

For an organization to apply ISO 27001 and effectively secure data, it must meet the 7 sections or "clauses" essential to protecting its information's confidentiality, integrity, and availability. Here is how the Plan-Do-Check-Act (PDCA) cycle relates to the clauses of ISO 27001.

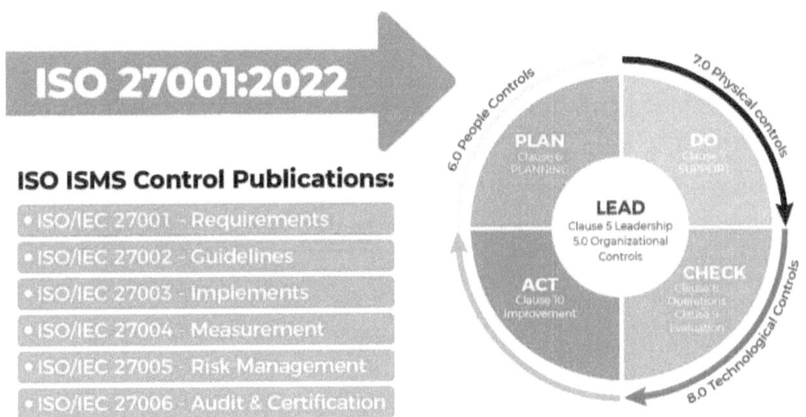

Lead

Before the PDCA can start, the organization must approve the security concepts of the ISO 27001 information security management system. Two clauses address this:

Clause 4: Context of the organization

> This involves identifying and assessing the factors impacting the organization's ability to achieve its information security objectives. Organizations can identify and assess the risks associated with their ISMS by understanding the internal and external context. Understanding the needs and expectations of other stakeholders and interested parties can help determine the scope of the ISMS in the context of a particular organization.

Clause 5: Leadership

ISO 27001 Requirement 5.1 explains that the organization's top management must demonstrate leadership and commitment to the ISMS. An information security policy must also be in place and approved by the top management. Organizational roles, responsibilities, and authorities must be clearly defined and assigned to ensure commitment and accountability.

Plan

An information security management system requires a plan.

Clause 6: Planning for Risk Management

ISO 27001 requires that organizations identify, assess, treat, and monitor information security risks and opportunities. Specific, measurable, achievable, relevant, and time-bound information security objectives should align with the organization's overall business objectives. A comprehensive plan to achieve these objectives must also be developed. Regular reviews of these objectives and plans are also necessary to ensure relevance.

Do

Once a plan is formed and backed by the leadership, it must be implemented.

Clause 7: Allocation of Resources

Allocation of resources can sometimes be challenging as allocating full-time resources to maintain the standard is not feasible. Instead, the clause states that specific team members of your organization take ownership of implementing the security and policy requirements listed in the ISMS. And that the employees tasked with this should be given access to training resources. Maintaining the ISMS should become part of the everyday or ongoing responsibilities of the team or individual. This ensures that maintenance becomes a core priority.

Clause 8: Regular Assessments and Evaluations of Operational Controls

Ongoing assessments and continuous evaluations of the implemented controls and policies are defined in this clause. This ensures that the ISMS functions optimally and that all the controls are sensible concerning the threat landscape. Any improvements identified in the evaluations can then be implemented. These evaluations and improvements must be documented to provide evidence of ongoing compliance.

Check

Once the ISMS is implemented, it needs to be monitored and evaluated.

Clause 9: Performance evaluation

Performance evaluations are also an excellent guide when conducting internal and external audits. During internal audits, these evaluations can be used to assess the effectiveness of the ISMS. An external auditor can also use these performance evaluations to assess whether your organization has implemented the necessary controls and policies and map them to your ISMS scope.

Act

Continuous monitoring allows improvement.

Clause 10: Improvement

With this ongoing evaluation, if any correction, improvement, or nonconformity is identified, it needs to be documented, and a plan to cover this gap needs to be put in place along with measurable objectives for achieving it. The plan should be prioritized, and timelines should be established to ensure the improvement is implemented within an acceptable timeframe.

The PDCA cycle is a dynamic model that ISO 27001 utilizes to improve the ISMS continually. Each clause within ISO 27001 fits into one of the stages of PDCA, ensuring a structured and continuous approach to managing and improving information security.

Remember this PDCA process throughout this book and consider how it aligns with the clauses.

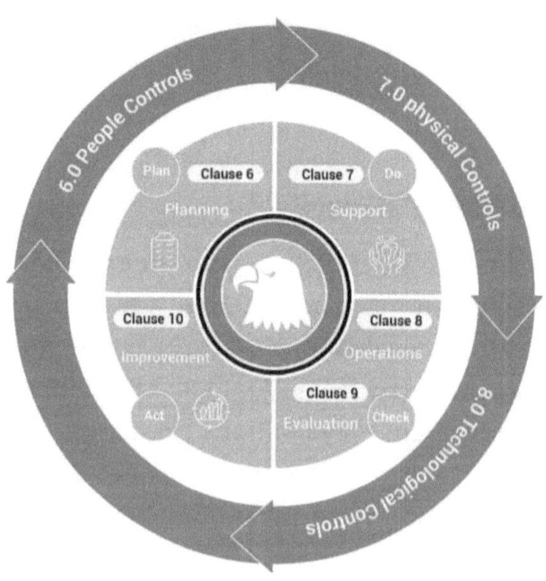

Chapter 2

LEAD – Managing the Information Security System

An ISO 27001 leader is a hero. The living embodiment of bravery. They blaze a trail that few dare even think to venture into. Throughout the centuries, scholars worldwide have studied their prowess on the battlefield and in the bedroom. But none can understand what makes them so far beyond the average human. Perhaps it is the ability to love. Whatever the reason, one thing is clear: we are blessed to live on the same planet as one, which is so true. For only by the grace of a higher power can anything be so sacred as this leader of the chosen.

– Direct Quote from an ISO 27001 Leader

(Source: Self-portrait of an ISO 27001 Leader)

All kidding aside, the organization's leadership involvement is foundational for successfully implementing an information security management system (ISMS). Management's role goes beyond budget control; they also guide the organization's mission and business direction.

Adding ISO 27001 security requires a cultural shift within the organization, affecting how people, processes, and technology operate. This means altering certain organizational habits, which demands comprehensive support from leadership.

ISO 27001 requires leadership's endorsement of the ISMS. Clauses 4 and 5 of the standards specifically address this aspect. Clause 4 focuses on understanding the organization's position in the broader context, while Clause 5 emphasizes leadership's support for the ISMS. These clauses form the foundation for effectively implementing ISO 27001 in any organization.

Clause 4 Context of the Organization

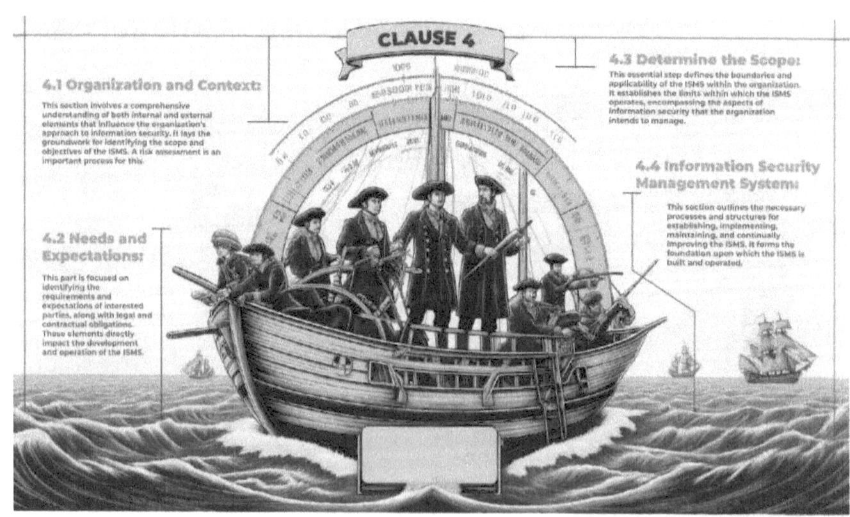

"Knowing yourself is the beginning of all wisdom."

-- Aristotle

The main takeaway of Clause 4 is that the organization must know itself. They need to understand what they provide, their value and impact on those they serve, and all the main tasks that make them capable of their mission and business.

Clause 4 is about understanding the environment in which the organization operates, including its specific challenges and opportunities, to ensure that the ISMS is aligned with the organization's overall goals and objectives

If the context of the organization is understood, it is easier to determine what needs to be protected and which effective strategies are helpful for information security. Clause 4 has the following subsections:

- **Organization and Context:** This section involves a comprehensive understanding of internal and external elements that influence the organization's approach to information security. It lays the groundwork for identifying the scope and objectives of the ISMS. A risk assessment is an important process for this.

- **Needs and Expectations:** This part is focused on identifying the requirements and expectations of interested parties, along with legal and contractual obligations. These elements directly impact the development and operation of the ISMS.

- **Determine the Scope:** This essential step defines the boundaries and applicability of the ISMS within the organization. It establishes the limits within which the ISMS operates, encompassing the aspects of information security that the organization intends to manage.

🖳 **Information Security Management System:** This section outlines the processes and structures for establishing, implementing, maintaining, and continually improving the ISMS. It forms the foundation upon which the ISMS is built and operated.

Clause 4.1 Understanding the Organization and its Context

The phrase "Context of the Organization" in ISO 27001 refers to knowing the internal and external factors that influence an organization's objectives, stakeholders, and the operation of its ISMS. Internal factors are elements within the organization that influence performance and decisions. For example:

- 🖳 Culture
- 🖳 Organizational structure
- 🖳 Internal resources
- 🖳 Policy and procedure
- 🖳 Inside threats & weaknesses

External factors are things outside the organization that could impact the operations:

- 🖳 Industry of the organization
- 🖳 Regulations and Laws
- 🖳 External threats
- 🖳 Social & cultural trends
- 🖳 Technological advances

Identifying these factors is crucial for tailoring the ISMS to the specific needs and conditions of the organization.

Understanding the organizational context is important for all decision-makers. "Decision-makers" include, but are not limited to, supervisors, managers, C-Level execs, leaders, or even regular employees making day-to-day choices that could affect the organization.

Clause 5.4.1 of ISO 31000:2018, which covers the risk assessment process in detail, is an excellent guide for understanding Clause 4 of ISO 27001:2022. This clause helps organizations set up a thorough process for assessing and managing risks, ensuring that the approach to handling risks matches the organization's strategy and main goals.

Clause 4.2 Understanding the Needs and Expectations of Interested Parties

Under Clause 4.2 of the ISO 27001:2022, an organization must understand its business environment and mission by identifying all relevant stakeholders.

Stakeholders are entities or individuals who have an interest in or influence on the organization's operations. These can include customers, employees, suppliers, and regulatory bodies. Their expectations and requirements help shape the ISMS, ensuring it secures information and aligns with the organization's broader objectives.

The organization needs to do the following for Clause 4.2:

- **Identification of Stakeholders (4.2a):** Determine who the stakeholders are.

- **Understanding Stakeholder Requirements (4.2b):** Ascertain what these stakeholders expect or require from the organization.

- **Aligning Stakeholder Requirements with the ISMS (4.2c):** Evaluate which requirements can be directly addressed through the ISMS.

Here are examples illustrating how stakeholders might be identified, their requirements, and the corresponding ISMS responses:

- **Customer Stakeholder:**

  - **Requirement:** Protection of their privacy; restrict access to sensitive information.

  - **ISMS Response:** Implement a Personally Identifiable Information (PII) policy; Elevate access rights to configure and maintain systems.

- **System Administrator:**

  - **Requirement:** Need for employee training in information security.

  - **ISMS Response:** Establishment of an IT On-the-Job Training (OJT) process.

- **Industry Auditor:**

  - **Requirement:** Compliance with relevant regulatory standards; implement role-based access controls (RBAC) to ensure system administrators have the necessary access to do work.

  - **ISMS Response:** Obtain ISO 27001 certification and conduct internal assessments.

By identifying stakeholders and understanding their specific needs, an organization can ensure that its ISMS is compliant, secure, and supportive of its larger goals and objectives. This alignment is essential for the success of the ISMS within the organization's framework. Additionally, a detailed and well-communicated understanding of these aspects contributes significantly to the overall effectiveness and relevance of the ISMS.

Clause 4.3 Determining the Scope of the ISMS

Clause 4.3 of ISO/IEC 27001:2022 focuses on defining the scope of the Information Security Management System (ISMS). For the ISMS to be effective, it's crucial to establish clear boundaries that delineate where information security measures are applicable within the organization.

The organization determines the scope of its ISMS by considering the following:

- **External and Internal Issues (4.3a)**: This includes understanding the organization's context, such as legal, technological, competitive, market, cultural, social, and economic environments, both internally and externally.

- **Stakeholder Requirements (4.3b)**: This involves considering the needs and expectations of interested parties and legal and regulatory requirements.

- **Interfaces and Dependencies (4.3c)**: This includes evaluating the relationships and interactions between internal activities and those outsourced or handled by other organizations.

By thoroughly assessing these aspects, an organization can effectively define the scope of its ISMS, ensuring comprehensive coverage and alignment with its overall objectives and context."

Clause 4.4 Establishing an Information Security Management System

Under Clause 4.4 of ISO/IEC 27001:2022, organizations must establish, implement, maintain, and continually improve an Information Security Management System (ISMS). This involves a comprehensive approach:

- **Establishing the ISMS**: Developing a framework that aligns with the organization's objectives, identifies potential risks, and outlines the necessary security controls.

🔲 **Implementing the ISMS**: Implementing the policies, procedures, and controls defined in the ISMS framework.

🔲 **Maintaining the ISMS**: Regular monitoring and upkeep of the ISMS to ensure its ongoing effectiveness in managing information security risks.

🔲 **Continually Improving the ISMS**: Adopting a proactive approach to refine and enhance the ISMS, responding to changes in the risk environment, technological advancements, and business processes.

This process includes identifying and managing the various processes needed for effective information security and understanding how these processes interact within the organizational context. Organizations must align these efforts with the specific requirements outlined in ISO/IEC 27001:2022, which include compliance with legal and regulatory obligations, meeting stakeholder expectations, and achieving strategic objectives.

By adhering to these guidelines, organizations can ensure a robust and responsive ISMS that protects against information security threats and supports and enhances overall business operations.

Clause 5 Leadership

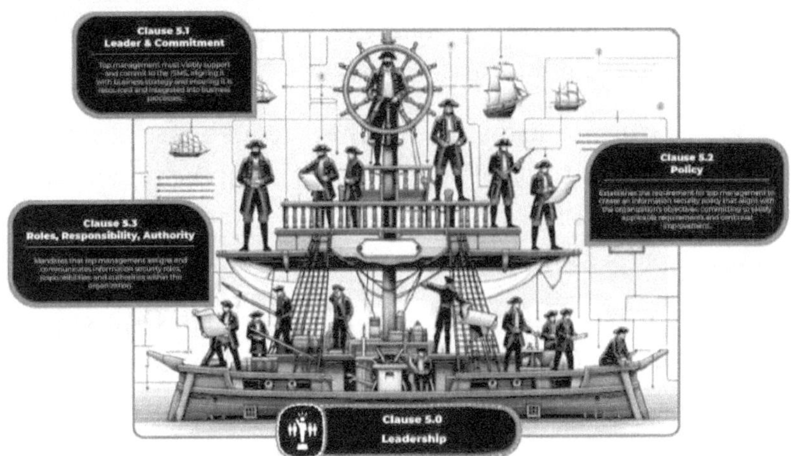

As a security worker trying to implement policies, it can be very frustrating when you get pushback from the organization. People (especially the IT department) hate security workers because we make them jump through additional hoops to do their jobs with security in mind.

Believe it or not, in the 90s, many systems didn't even have passwords! Or they had shared passwords because it was easier. You should have seen how PISSED people got when they were forced to use individual passwords that changed every few months.

Without backing from leadership, it feels impossible to get any security processes to stick.

Clause 5 focuses on leadership. It brings up the importance of management in implementing the ISO 27001. This clause addresses the distribution of roles and responsibilities and the full backing of upper management of the ISMS. Clause 5 has the following subsections:

5.1 Leadership and Commitment: Top management must visibly support and commit to the ISMS, aligning it with business strategy and ensuring it is resourced and integrated into business processes.

5.2 Policy: Establishes the requirement for top management to create an information security policy that aligns with the organization's objectives, committing to satisfy applicable requirements and continual improvement.

5.3 Organizational Roles, Responsibilities, and Authorities: This mandates that top management assign and communicate information security roles, responsibilities, and authorities within the organization.

Clause 5.1 Leadership and Commitment

The full endorsement and active involvement of leadership means having a strategy that addresses the who, what, when, why, and how of the organizational ISMS.

Clause 5.1 has sub-sections that break down what leaders are supposed to do:

- **ISMS Security Policy (5.1a):** Upper-level management should ensure that the information security policy and objectives are aligned with the organization's strategic direction.

- **Integration into Organizational Processes (5.1b):** The requirements of the ISMS must be integrated into the organization's overall processes, ensuring that information security is not an isolated function but a part of the organizational fabric.

- **Resource Availability (5.1c):** Adequate resources must be provided for the ISMS. This includes everything from financial resources to personnel and technology.

- **Communication and Awareness (5.1d)**: There should be an active effort to communicate the importance of information security management. This includes ensuring the ISMS requirements are understood and upheld across the organization.

- **Achieving ISMS Outcomes (5.1e)**: The leadership must ensure that the ISMS achieves its intended outcomes, aligning with the organization's information security needs and objectives.

- **Support and Direction (5.1f)**: Top management should direct and support individuals in contributing to the effectiveness of the ISMS. This involves fostering a culture where every organization member understands their role in information security.

- **Promotion of Continual Improvement (5.1g)**: There should be a continual effort to improve the ISMS, adapting to changes in the internal and external context of the organization.

- **Support for Management Roles (5.1h)**: Leadership must support other relevant managerial roles, ensuring they can exhibit leadership concerning their responsibilities in the ISMS.

Clause 5 establishes that an ISMS's success largely depends on top management's leadership and commitment. By aligning the ISMS with the strategic direction, integrating it into organizational processes, ensuring resource availability, promoting continual improvement, and supporting roles at all levels, leadership can create a robust and effective ISMS. This clause underscores the idea that information security is not just a technical issue but a strategic and integral part of the organization.

Clause 5.2 Policy

Clause 5.2 focuses on the establishment of an information security policy. This policy is a fundamental element of the Information Security Management System (ISMS) and guides the organization's information security efforts.

Key Requirements of the Information Security Policy

Alignment with Organizational Purpose (5.2a):
The policy must be appropriate to the organization's purpose, reflecting its specific needs, goals, and context regarding information security.

Inclusion of Information Security Objectives (5.2b):
It should either directly include information security objectives or provide a framework for setting them, as detailed in Clause 6.2.

Commitment to Applicable Requirements (5.2c):
The policy must express a commitment to satisfy all applicable requirements related to information security. These may include legal, regulatory, contractual, or any other requirements the organization is subject to.

Commitment to Continual Improvement (5.2d):
A crucial component of the policy is the commitment to the continual improvement of the ISMS, ensuring that it remains effective and responsive to changes.

Dissemination and Accessibility of the Policy:

One thing that is clear in all the assessments I have had the misfortune of getting caught up in is that assessors don't care if you have never seen the organization's policy. But if the organization made an effort to make everyone aware of it, it shows.

Documented Information (5.2e):
The information security policy must be documented. This ensures clarity, consistency, and accessibility to everyone in the organization.

Internal Communication (5.2f):
The policy should be communicated within the organization. Every organization member should know the policy and understand its implications for their role.

Availability to Interested Parties (5.2g):
The policy should be available to interested parties as appropriate. This might include stakeholders, partners, clients, and regulatory bodies, depending on the nature of the organization and its activities.

Clause 5.2 establishes the requirements for an effective information security policy within an organization. This policy is a formal document and a cornerstone of the ISMS. It aligns with the organization's purpose, sets the tone for information security objectives, commits to satisfying applicable requirements, and pledges continual improvement of the ISMS. Its proper documentation, internal dissemination, and availability to relevant parties are crucial for the comprehensive and effective implementation of the ISMS.

Clause 5.3 Organizational Roles, Responsibilities, and Authorities

Clause 5.3 addresses assigning roles, responsibilities, and authorities within an organization's ISMS. It emphasizes the role of top management in ensuring that these elements are clearly defined, assigned, and communicated.

Assignment and Communication of Responsibilities and Authorities

Upper management is responsible for ensuring that the roles relevant to information security are clearly defined. This includes assigning specific responsibilities and authorities related to the ISMS.

These assignments must be effectively communicated within the organization. This clarity helps establish accountability and ensure that each role is carried out effectively.

The assignment and communication of responsibilities within an organization, according to the ISO 27001 standards, emphasize the importance of clear definition, assignment, and communication of roles relevant to information security. This clarity is crucial for establishing accountability and ensuring the effective execution of each role. Here are examples of specific responsibilities that can be assigned within an organization's ISMS:

- **Developing Information Security Policies:** Responsibilities include drafting, reviewing, and updating the organization's information security policies in line with its objectives, legal and regulatory requirements, and changes in the threat landscape.

- **Conducting Risk Assessments:** Identifying information assets, assessing risks to those assets, and conducting regular reviews of the risk landscape to identify any changes. This includes defining risk criteria, identifying threats, and determining the likelihood and impact of potential security incidents.

- **Implementing Risk Treatment Plans:** Once risks are identified, responsibilities include selecting appropriate risk options (avoidance, mitigation, transfer, or acceptance), implementing controls to manage identified risks, and monitoring the effectiveness of these controls.

- **Managing Information Security Incidents:** Responsibilities include establishing an incident response team, developing incident response plans, conducting regular incident response exercises, and managing actual incidents following the plan.

- **Ensuring Legal and Regulatory Compliance:** Identifying applicable legal, regulatory, and contractual requirements related to information security and ensuring that the organization complies with these requirements through appropriate controls and procedures.

- **Internal Audits:** Planning, conducting, and reporting on internal audits of the ISMS to ensure its effectiveness and compliance with ISO/IEC 27001 requirements. This includes selecting auditors, defining audit criteria, and managing follow-up actions from audit findings.

- **Awareness and Training:** Developing and implementing an information security awareness program to ensure that employees and relevant stakeholders know their information security responsibilities and provide specific training on information security risks and controls relevant to their roles.

- **Document and Record Control:** Managing documentation and records related to the ISMS, ensuring they are up-to-date, accessible, and protected against unauthorized access or modification.

- **Continual Improvement:** Identifying opportunities for improvement in the ISMS, managing the implementation of improvements, and monitoring their effectiveness.

These examples highlight the diverse responsibilities that must be assigned and communicated within an organization to ensure effective information security management.

Responsibility for Conformance to Standard's Requirements (5.3a):

There should be designated individuals responsible for ensuring that the ISMS conforms to the requirements outlined in ISO 27001:2022. This involves overseeing the implementation and maintenance of the ISMS according to the standard.

Reporting on ISMS Performance (5.3b):

Top management must assign the responsibility for reporting on the performance of the ISMS. This includes monitoring and reviewing the effectiveness of the ISMS and communicating this to top management.

Such reporting is critical for informed decision-making and the ISMS's continual improvement.

Delegation:

The standard indicates that senior management can assign duties and powers related to reporting the ISMS's effectiveness throughout the organization. This assignment should be carried out carefully to maintain the accuracy and effectiveness of the reports.

Clause 5.3 underscores the importance of clearly defined roles, responsibilities, and authorities in effectively managing an organization's ISMS. By assigning these roles and ensuring communication within the organization, top management can foster a strong security culture and ensure the ISMS complies with the standard and is effective in practice. This structured approach to role assignment and authority delegation is essential for the robust and efficient functioning of the ISMS.

Clause 5 ISO 27001 Information Security Controls

The synergy between understanding the organizational context (Clause 4) and demonstrating strong leadership (Clause 5) cannot be overstated. It's a blend of the practical aspects of understanding the organization's environment and the more abstract yet equally important elements of leadership and commitment.

By meticulously addressing these two clauses, organizations can lay a solid foundation for their ISMS compliant with ISO 27001 and resonate with their unique operational landscape and strategic goals.

There are ISO 27001:2022 organizational controls that pertain to Clause 5. These address the processes, policies, and procedures that must be backed and supported by the organization. They guide leadership in constructing an effective ISMS that fits the mission and business needs.

Here is a list of the relevant controls (for more details, see Chapter 7, Annex A Informational Security Controls):

5.1 Policies for Information Security

5.2 Information security roles and responsibilities

5.3 Segregation of duties

5.4 Management responsibilities

5.5 Contact with Authorities

5.6 Contact with special interest groups

5.7 Threat intelligence

5.30 ICT readiness for business continuity

5.31 Legal, statutory, regulatory and contractual requirements

5.32 Intellectual property rights

5.33 Protection of records

5.34 Privacy and protection of personal identifiable information (PII)

5.35 Independent review of information security

5.36 Compliance with policies, rules, and standards for information security

5.37 Documented operating procedures

Chapter 3

PLAN – Develop a Strategic Approach to Information Security

"A goal without a plan is just a wish."

- Antoine de Saint-Exupéry.

After the ISMS has the backing of the leadership and it is understood how it applies to the organization, the Plan-Do-Check-Act process can begin.

Some organizations place Clauses 4 & 5 into the "Plan" portion of the PDCA. This makes sense because you can't do planning effectively without them. In this book, we isolate Clause 6, "Planning," with the "Plan" part of the PDCA to get into greater detail.

Clause 6 Planning

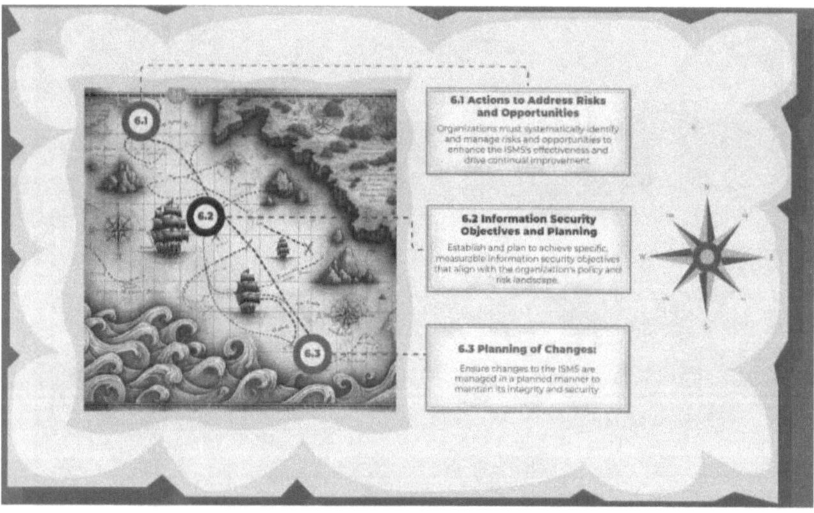

"Planning" pulls in data gathered from risk assessments, system and process weaknesses, and the business and mission requirements to design the information security management system.

You can see how planning depends on the actions of Clauses 4 and 5. Clause 4 gets all the business and mission requirements information necessary for planning, and Clause 5 provides the backing and buy-in of leadership.

Clause 6 includes the following:

- **6.1 Actions to Address Risks and Opportunities:** Organizations must systematically identify and manage risks and opportunities to enhance the ISMS's effectiveness and drive continual improvement.

- **6.2 Information Security Objectives and Planning to Achieve Them:** Establish and plan to achieve specific, measurable information security objectives that align with the organization's policy and risk landscape.

- **6.3 Planning of Changes:** Ensure changes to the ISMS are planned to maintain its integrity and security.

Clause 6.1.1 Actions to Address Risks and Opportunities

In this clause, the organization is guided to develop plans for its ISMS, considering the internal and external factors and stakeholder requirements outlined in Clause 4. The focus of these plans should be to ensure that the ISMS is effectively designed to do the following:

- **Achieve Intended Outcomes (6.1.1a):** The ISMS should be aligned with the organization's overall objectives, ensuring that it supports and enhances these goals.

- **Mitigate Threats (6.1.1b):** Proactive measures should be in place to prevent or minimize the impact of potential security threats.

- **Address Known Risks (6.1.1c):** The organization needs to identify, evaluate, and manage known risks to its information security.

- **Implement Actions and Responses to Risk (6.1.1d):** There should be a clear strategy for how the organization will respond to risks, including specific actions and procedures.

- **Review and Assess Risk Treatment and Actions (6.1.1e):** It's crucial to regularly evaluate the effectiveness of the risk treatment strategies and actions taken, making adjustments as necessary to improve the ISMS.

This comprehensive approach ensures that the organization's ISMS is robust, adaptable, and capable of addressing the ever-changing nature of information security risks.

Clause 6.1.2 Information Security Risk Assessment

Risk in information security is understood as the potential impact on the organization due to the exploitation of a vulnerability by a threat. Understanding these risks is essential to understanding the ISMS.

Risk Acceptance Criteria (6.1.2a & 6.1.2b)

The organization needs to define its information security risk criteria; this involves determining what security risks are acceptable and how information risk assessments will be performed.

For example, the organization might deem 'low' risk-to the public website as 'acceptable' if leadership approves this in a "risk acceptance" document. Additionally, the organization might mandate that all information security risk assessments be conducted by the "Risk Assessment Department" using approved security scanners. Similarly, assessments of all physical security risks might be required by the "Site Security Team."

I have been exposed to many different organizations' information security management programs, and each has a different level of risk they are willing to take and a different way of handling assessments. There is no one-size-fits-all solution.

What is common among good ISMS is that the organization will ensure that security risk assessments produce consistent, reliable results that can be repeated. Another mark of a great ISMS is that the risk acceptance criteria are agreed on, documented, and approved.

Conducting a risk assessment is an effective way to comprehend risks, threats, vulnerabilities, and potential impacts. This process involves identifying, analyzing, and evaluating risks.

Risk Identification (6.1.2c)

The initial step for any organization is to clarify its objectives. What is the mission or business goal, and what factors contribute to its success? Key elements include the people, processes, and technology driving the mission and business. An important aspect of risk identification involves understanding the potential threats to these elements.

Leaders must be well-informed about their industry and their organization's specific threats. Different industries are susceptible to different risks. For example, an international retail chain might prioritize the threat of credit card information theft from point-of-sale systems. In contrast, a manufacturing firm or science laboratory might focus more on preventing leaks of proprietary information.

Describing risks, including their sources and potential consequences, is essential in achieving the organization's objectives. Familiarity with the industry aids in this process. Leaders can begin by obtaining industry-focused risk reports.

Risk Analysis (6.1.2d)

This stage is about assessing the nature and level of identified risks. It involves understanding the risk, its causes, likelihood, and potential impact. A critical question for each identified risk is, "What would impact our mission or business if this threat materializes?"

Key factors in risk analysis include:

- **Asset Value**: Evaluation of the criticality and value of the information assets to the organization. This helps prioritize risks based on the significance of the asset affected.

- **Threat Capability**: Assessing the capability of potential threat actors to exploit vulnerabilities. This involves considering the resources, skills, and motivation of potential attackers.

- **Control Effectiveness**: Evaluating the current security controls' effectiveness in mitigating identified risks. This includes both technical and administrative controls.

- **Impact Severity**: Detailed assessment of the severity of the impact, considering both quantitative (financial loss, downtime duration) and qualitative (reputational damage, legal consequences) factors.

- **Risk Interdependencies**: Understanding how individual risks are interrelated and how the materialization of one risk could impact or trigger other risks.

Enhancing the Risk Analysis Process:

- **Use of Risk Assessment Frameworks and Methodologies**: Leveraging established risk assessment frameworks (e.g., OCTAVE, FAIR) to provide a structured approach to risk analysis.

- **Stakeholder Involvement**: Engaging with stakeholders across different levels and functions of the organization to gain a comprehensive view of risks and impacts. This includes IT, business units, legal, and human resources.

- **Scenario Analysis**: Conducting scenario-based analysis to understand the potential outcomes of risk events, including worst-case scenarios. This aids in visualizing the impact and preparing more effectively.

- **Quantitative Risk Analysis Techniques**: Where appropriate, apply quantitative methods (e.g., annual loss expectancy calculation) to assign monetary values to risks, aiding in prioritization and decision-making.

- **Regular Review and Updating**: Risk analysis is not a one-time activity but a continuous process. Regularly reviewing and updating the risk analysis to reflect changes in the threat landscape, vulnerabilities, and business context.

These factors contribute to a thorough risk analysis.

Risk Evaluation (6.1.2e)

Risk evaluation involves comparing the analysis results with clear, predefined standards to determine if the risk severity is acceptable. These predefined standards may include:

- **Risk Appetite:** The overall level of risk the organization is comfortable taking to achieve its goals.

- **Risk Tolerance:** Specific limits on how much risk the organization can handle, like financial caps.

- **Compliance Requirements:** Rules and regulations that the organization must follow.

- **Alignment with Goals:** How the risk fits the organization's primary objectives.

- **Impact Levels:** Set points for different types of impacts, such as money loss or damage to reputation.

- **Likelihood Levels:** What chance of the risk happening is acceptable?

- **Cost-Benefit Analysis:** Comparing the potential gains of an opportunity against the risks involved.

- **Risk Capacity:** The highest level of risk the organization can take without serious problems.

After completing the risk analysis, the organization must decide how to deal with these risks based on this evaluation. This is known as risk treatment or risk response.

Clause 6.1.3 Information Security Risk Treatment

The organization needs to define the risk treatment (also known as risk response). This is important because not all vulnerabilities can be fixed immediately, and there are many levels of risk. Risk treatments give the organization the flexibility to address risks regardless of what they are.

Selection of Risk Treatment Options (6.1.3a)

The organization needs to define and apply an information security risk treatment process. This is crucial because not all vulnerabilities can be addressed immediately, and risks vary in severity. Implementing risk treatments provides the organization with the flexibility to address a range of risks effectively:

- **Remediation:** The process of completely removing the vulnerability or threat from the organization. Patching, reconfiguring, and updating are great examples of how an organization can fix or "remediate" a known issue.

- **Avoidance:** Avoiding the risk entirely, often by not engaging in the activity that generates the risk. A company might implement a strict policy that prevents employees from downloading and installing any software from the internet on their work devices. This approach directly avoids the risk of malware infections from untrusted or malicious websites. The company might enforce this by using network-level controls to block access to software download sites or set administrative privileges that restrict software installation.

- **Reduction or Mitigation:** Implementing controls or actions to reduce the likelihood or impact of the risk. An example would be a company installing anti-virus software on all workstations and regularly updating it to protect against known malware. They also conduct frequent cybersecurity training sessions for employees to help them recognize phishing attempts and unsafe websites. This combination of technical measures and user education reduces the risk of malware infections and minimizes the impact should an infection occur.

- **Transfer:** Shifting the risk to another party, often through insurance or outsourcing. A company might purchase a cyber insurance policy covering data breach costs, including legal fees, notification costs, and credit monitoring for affected individuals. Alternatively, they might outsource their email security to a cloud-based service provider specialized in identifying and filtering phishing and spam emails, transferring some of the risks of email-based malware.

- **Acceptance:** Acknowledging the risk and deciding not to take action to change its likelihood or impact. This is usually chosen when the cost of treating the risk outweighs the potential benefit. After assessing its cybersecurity posture, a small business decides that the cost of advanced cybersecurity measures exceeds the potential benefit, given its low-risk profile and limited exposure to sensitive information. They accept the risk of a malware infection, focusing instead on maintaining basic security practices and planning to address any incidents reactively. This doesn't mean they ignore cybersecurity; they accept that some risks are tolerable within their business strategy.

- **Action Plan:** In cases where the organization cannot reduce or mitigate a known vulnerability in a timely manner, they can implement a plan to track the actions that will be used to fix the issue. This is a documented process where the team meets on a regular basis until the issues are resolved.

These are just the most common risk treatment options. An organization can develop its own or use some variation of the ones listed. It's important to document and monitor the work done.

Controls Necessary to Implement Risk Treatment (6.1.3b)

In accordance with ISO/IEC 27001:2022, the organization must determine all controls necessary to implement the chosen information security risk treatment options. This step is crucial in ensuring the risk treatment is effectively applied and aligned with the risk assessment findings.

Compare the Controls in 6.1.3 with Annex A (6.1.3c)

It's important to compare the determined controls with those listed in Annex A (listed in ISO 27001 and in this book) to ensure that no essential controls are missed. Annex A provides a comprehensive list of possible information security controls, which is not exhaustive, allowing for the inclusion of additional controls as required.

It's important to compare the determined controls with those listed in Annex A of the standard to ensure no essential controls are missed. This comparison serves several key purposes:

Ensuring Completeness: By comparing the selected controls with Annex A, the organization can verify that all necessary controls have been considered. Annex A serves as a comprehensive checklist against which the organization's chosen controls can be validated.

Identifying Gaps: This comparison can reveal gaps in the organization's current control strategy, highlighting areas requiring additional attention or different controls.

Enhancing the Control Strategy: The exercise may also identify additional controls from Annex A that could strengthen the organization's risk treatment approach.

Customization to Specific Needs: While Annex A provides a broad range of controls, each organization's context is unique. This step allows for customization of the control set to fit specific operational and risk profiles.

Here is a brief step-by-step approach as to how this comparison can be carried out:

- **List the Selected Controls:** Start by listing all the controls that the organization has identified and selected as part of its risk treatment strategy.

- **Review Annex A:** Carefully review Annex A, which contains a comprehensive list of possible information security controls.

- **Conduct a Comparative Analysis:** Match each selected control against those in Annex A. Note where there is alignment and where there are differences.

- **Identify Gaps and Overlaps:** Look for gaps where Annex A suggests controls that have not been considered. Also, note any overlaps where your selected controls might cover multiple aspects listed in Annex A.

- **Adjust Control Strategy as Needed:** Based on the comparative analysis, adjust the control strategy to fill gaps, remove redundancies, or enhance controls for better risk management.

- **Document the Comparison:** Keep a record of this comparison and the rationale for the final selection of controls. This documentation is crucial for audits and reviews.

Annex A is not exhaustive, meaning organizations can and should include additional information security controls as needed, tailoring them to their specific risk landscape.

Produce a Statement of Applicability (6.1.3d)

The process involves producing a Statement of Applicability (SOA). This statement should include justifications for the inclusion and implementation status of the necessary controls and explain why any controls from Annex A are excluded. This step provides clarity and transparency in the risk treatment process.

Formulate Risk Treatment Plan (6.1.3e & 6.1.3f)

Formulating a risk treatment plan is a key step, which should be followed by obtaining approval for the plan and their acceptance of the residual information security risks.

- **Implementation of Treatment Plans:** After selecting the most appropriate treatment option(s), the next step is implementing the necessary measures. This could involve changes in processes, policies, or the use of technology.

- **Monitoring and Review:** Risk treatment is not a one-time action. It requires ongoing monitoring and review to ensure the measures are effective and to make adjustments as the business environment or the nature of the risks changes.

Risk treatment is a key component of risk management, particularly in information security, where it's essential to balance the need to protect information with the practicalities of running an organization. Once created, obtain risk owners' approval of the information security risk treatment plan and acceptance of the residual information security risks. The organization shall retain documented information about the information security risk treatment process. These documents should be stored in a secure repository accessible to authorized personnel who need it.

Clause 6.2 Information Security Objectives and Planning

ISMS is designed to establish specific information security objectives across all relevant functions and levels, ensuring a comprehensive approach to protecting information confidentiality, integrity, and availability. These objectives are tailored to the organization's unique context, reflecting its specific needs, size, nature, and the security risks it faces. In alignment with ISO/IEC 27001:2022, the organization commits to a detailed planning process to effectively achieve these objectives, outlining the actions, resources, responsibilities, timelines, and evaluation methods to ensure successful implementation and continual improvement.

Security Objectives Aligned with Security Policy (6.2a)

The information security objectives must be consistent with the security policy. The information security policy will cover every part of the organization's business and mission. This ensures that all security features fall under the security policy.

The organization's information security objectives are crafted to align fully with the overarching information security policy. This alignment ensures a cohesive approach to safeguarding the confidentiality, integrity, and availability of information across all facets of the organization's operations and mission-critical functions. By integrating security objectives under the umbrella of the security policy, the organization guarantees that each security initiative and control contributes directly to the overarching goals of information security, as outlined in the policy. This strategic alignment facilitates a comprehensive and coherent implementation of security measures tailored to the specific needs and context of the organization.

Measurable Information Security Objectives (6.2b)

When practical, the security of the ISMS should be measurable. For example, some organizations apply a number or a mathematical algorithm to cyber security risks based on how many weaknesses are remediated and the likelihood of threats exploiting known weaknesses. This is a quantitative rather than a qualitative approach to determining the effectiveness of security objectives.

A qualitative approach to information security enables the organization to systematically assess performance against objectives, identify areas for improvement, and demonstrate compliance with information security requirements. This approach can be applied to risk assessments, incident response metrics, compliance, and security training ratings.

Consideration of Security Requirements and Risk Assessment/Treatment (6.2c)

The organization must ensure its information security objectives reflect applicable legal, regulatory, and contractual requirements. This involves integrating the outcomes of risk assessments and risk treatment processes into the objectives. The organization aligns its security efforts with external expectations and internal risk management strategy, ensuring a comprehensive approach to safeguarding information security.

Monitoring of Objectives (6.2d)

The organization is required to actively monitor its information security objectives to assess their relevance, effectiveness, and achievement. Monitoring enables the identification of trends, effectiveness of controls, and areas needing improvement or adjustment. This ongoing scrutiny ensures that the ISMS remains dynamic and responsive to changing internal and external environments.

Communication of Objectives (6.2e)

Information security objectives must be communicated within the organization to ensure all members understand their individual and collective roles in achieving their goals. Clear communication helps align efforts, foster a culture of security, and ensure that security practices are integrated into daily operations.

Updating Objectives (6.2f)

The organization should periodically review and update its information security objectives to reflect changes in the risk landscape, business direction, or external requirements. This ensures that the ISMS remains aligned with the organization's current needs and goals and maintains its effectiveness over time.

Documentation of Objectives (6.2g)

The organization must maintain documented information regarding its information security objectives. This documentation serves as a reference point for planning, implementing, and evaluating security measures and provides evidence of the organization's commitment to continuous improvement in information security management.

Moving forward to the planning section, where the organization outlines its approach to achieving these objectives:

Action Planning (6.2h)

The organization must determine the specific actions required to achieve its information security objectives. This involves outlining the strategies, processes, or activities to be undertaken, ensuring a structured approach to enhancing its ISMS.

Resource Allocation (6.2i)

Identifying and providing the necessary human, technological, and financial resources is essential for achieving information security objectives. This ensures that the ISMS has the support to implement and maintain effectively.

Responsibility Assignment (6.2j)

The organization must assign responsibilities to achieve its information security objectives. By designating specific individuals or teams with these tasks, the organization ensures accountability and facilitates effective management of its security measures.

Timeframe Determination (6.2k)

Determining when each information security objective should be completed is crucial for timely and effective implementation. This helps prioritize actions and ensures the organization maintains momentum in its continuous improvement efforts.

Evaluation of Results (6.2l)

Finally, the organization must determine how the results of its efforts toward achieving information security objectives will be evaluated. This involves establishing metrics or criteria for success and implementing mechanisms for measuring performance against these benchmarks. This evaluation feeds into continuous improvement, ensuring the ISMS evolves to meet emerging challenges.

Each component plays a vital role in ensuring that the organization's information security objectives are well-defined, aligned with broader goals, and effectively implemented, monitored, and adapted over time.

Clause 6.3 Planning of changes

When the organization determines the need for changes to the information security management system, the changes shall be planned.

There is a need to incorporate a structured change management process into the ISMS to ensure that changes are controlled and secure. By planning changes carefully, organizations can enhance their security posture, meet evolving business and compliance requirements, and foster an environment of continuous improvement within their information security management system. Some organizations use the following methods for dealing with change management.

- **Change Identification and Initiation**: Any change to the ISMS should start with clearly identifying and defining the change. This includes understanding the need for change, the specific elements of the ISMS that will be affected, and the objectives the change aims to achieve.

- **Impact Assessment**: Before implementing any changes, thoroughly assess the potential effects on the ISMS and the organization's security posture. This assessment should consider the implications for risk levels, compliance with legal and regulatory requirements, and the potential impacts on stakeholders.

- **Planning and Designing the Change**: Develop a detailed plan for implementing the change, including the steps required, resources needed, roles and responsibilities, and a timeline. The plan should also include measures for mitigating any identified risks associated with the change.

- **Approval Process**: Establish a formal approval process for changes, ensuring relevant stakeholders review and authorize all changes before implementation. This process should include criteria for evaluating proposed changes' necessity and potential impact.

- **Implementation and Monitoring**: Implement the change according to the plan, with continuous monitoring to detect any issues that arise during the process. Effective communication throughout the implementation phase ensures that all relevant parties are informed and prepared for the change.

- ⚙ **Review and Post-Implementation Evaluation**: After implementing a change, conduct a review to evaluate the effectiveness of the change and its alignment with the initial objectives. This review should also identify any unintended consequences or additional risks the change introduces and recommend corrective actions if necessary.

- ⚙ **Documentation and Continuous Improvement**: Document all changes made to the ISMS, including the rationale for the change, the impact assessment, the implementation process, and the review findings. This documentation supports continuous improvement by providing insights into the change management process and its outcomes.

Clause 6 ISO 27001 Information Security Controls

Clause 6 is all about proactive planning. It emphasizes the need for organizations to be aware of their specific context, to identify risks and opportunities, and to take deliberate actions to enhance their ISMS. By doing so, organizations protect their information more effectively and pave the way for continuous improvement in their security practices.

Here is a list of the relevant controls that help the planning by managing the people in the ISMS process (for more details, see Chapter 7, Annex A, Informational Security Controls):

6.1 Screening

6.2 Terms and conditions of employment

6.3 Information security awareness, education, and training

6.4 Disciplinary process

6.5 Responsibilities after termination or change of employment

6.6 Confidentiality or non-disclosure agreements

6.7 Remote working

6.8 Information security event reporting

Chapter 4

DO – Conducting the ISMS

A great and terrifying man once said, "Everyone has a plan until they get punched in the mouth."

I think he was trying to say that a plan is not enough. The organization has to take action and to do so; it needs support and consideration of actual operations.

With a solid plan and leadership backing, implementation is the next crucial step in ISO 27001 compliance. This chapter explores how Clauses 7 and 8 of ISO 27001 guide organizations in effectively executing and maintaining ISMS.

Clause 7 Support

The successful implementation of an information security management system starts with the strategic allocation of resources. Clause 7 recognizes that not all organizations can dedicate full-time resources to the ISMS and advocates for a flexible approach. Organizations should identify specific roles or departments where ISMS responsibilities can be expanded to encompass ISMS duties. For example, IT, compliance, or rissoles roles could be expanded to encompass ISMS duties.

To support this integration, organizations should establish clear guidelines on distributing resources such as budget, time, and personnel. For instance, a small or medium-sized enterprise might allocate a percentage of an IT manager's time to ISMS duties, supplemented with periodic consultations from external experts. Clause 7 has the following sub-clauses:

- **Clause 7.1 Resources:** This requires the organization to allocate the necessary resources to establish, implement, maintain, and continually improve its information security management system.

- **Clause 7.2 Competence:** Ensures personnel are competent in information security based on the security controls.

- **Clause 7.3 Awareness:** Has the organization raised awareness of information security requirements among its personnel?

- **Clause 7.4 Communication:** Has the organization established internal communication processes for information security matters?

- **Clause 7.5 Documented Information:** The organization must create and maintain documented information to support the operation of its ISMS.

Clause 7.1 Resources

The organization must conduct a thorough assessment to determine the specific resources needed for the ISMS implementation. This includes identifying the personnel, technology, and financial resources required. For instance, a detailed resource plan could outline the need for cybersecurity software, additional staff training, or even new hires. The plan should align with the organization's context, stakeholder expectations, and the risks identified in the ISMS risk assessment process.

Clause 7.2 Competence

Leadership is vital in ensuring that personnel are equipped with the necessary skills and undergo continuous training, particularly in crucial areas such as risk assessment. To effectively integrate an ISMS into the organizational fabric, it's essential to incorporate security considerations into daily operations, including project management processes, and to keep staff regularly informed about security topics. This integration creates a culture where information security is a natural part of the organizational culture. The ongoing evaluation and timely adaptation of the ISMS are essential to address the rapidly changing landscape of security threats and business dynamics, underlining the need for a commitment to continuous improvement.

Necessary People (7.2a)

Leadership must define the skills and competence levels of individuals implementing the ISMS. This involves creating a competence matrix that details required skills, such as risk assessment proficiency, knowledge of specific security protocols, and desired experience levels.

Training (7.2b, 7.2c, 7.2d)

To ensure ongoing competence, a structured training program should be implemented. This program could include annual cybersecurity workshops, e-learning courses, and attendance at relevant conferences. Maintaining records such as training certificates, performance reviews, and job descriptions as evidence of competence is also important.

Integrating ISMS into Organizational Culture

The ISMS should be linked with everyday business processes and decision-making to embed information security into the organizational culture. For example, integrating ISMS considerations into project management frameworks or including security metrics in departmental performance reviews can reinforce its importance. Regular communication, such as security newsletters or briefings, can keep staff engaged and aware of security issues.

Continuous Improvement and Adaptation

Organizations should adopt a mindset of continuous improvement in managing their ISMS. This involves regular reviews of resource allocation, competence levels, and the integration of ISMS into the organizational culture, as well as adjusting strategies to address emerging threats and changes in the business environment.

Clause 7.3 Awareness

This clause emphasizes the importance of making employees aware of the information security policy, their roles in the ISMS, the benefits of improved information security, and the consequences of non-compliance.

The organization will distribute and publicize the information security policy. They can do this in many ways (7.3ba):

- Having all new employees review the policy
- Sending the policy to all employees via email
- Training based on policy
- Annual security policy refresher

Workers need to be aware of their role in the ISMS. This includes how they're tasked with helping to secure information (7.3b).

Non-conformance with Policy (7.3c)

The organization will develop and implement rules for addressing non-compliance with the security policies. They will define the actions that constitute non-conformance, such as failure to follow security protocols, improper use of sensitive information, or neglect to complete required security training. The organization will set up the consequences for breaking the rules.

Some examples of organizational responses for non-compliance with policy include:

- Verbal / written warning
- Mandatory security awareness training
- Access limitation
- Suspension
- Termination
- Legal action

In my experience, the most non-compliance is from employees, and it is simple things like improper password protection, missing security training, downloading unapproved software, and stuff like that. The organization usually uses verbal or written reminders or mandatory security awareness. The punishments fit the impact of the crime.

Clause 7.4 Communication

This clause addresses the necessity for effective internal and external communication regarding the ISMS. Effective communication entails understanding what to communicate, when to do it, how, and with whom.

What to Communicate (7.4a)

Some aspects of the ISMS are mainly dependent on clear communication, including:

- **Incident response:** Detailing the steps and responsibilities during a security incident.

- **Vulnerability management:** Sharing information about identified vulnerabilities and how to address them.

- **Cyberthreat intelligence:** Disseminating knowledge about potential or emerging cyber threats.

When to Communicate (7.4b)

The organization must establish regular communication schedules to ensure all stakeholders are informed and aligned. Configuration management meetings could be a platform for regular communication. However, immediate communication is imperative to address and mitigate risks in specific scenarios, such as security incidents.

Whom to Communicate With (7.4c)

The target audience for communication depends on the nature and purpose of the information being shared. The organization should maintain a roster of relevant stakeholders for various types of communications. For example:

- Security breaches, mishaps, attacks, and other security incidents typically require immediate communication with an incident response team.

- Discussions about vulnerabilities and their remediation may need dialogue with vendors or external security experts.

- Updates or changes in security policies or procedures should be communicated to all employees and relevant external parties to ensure widespread awareness and compliance.

How to Communicate (7.4d)

Some communication is done internally with meetings, bulletins, and emails. External communications must be done with security in mind. Here are a few situations where communication is needed and how it might be done.

Internal Effective Communication Channels:

- **Regular ISMS Review Meetings**: Establish regular meetings to discuss the status and updates of the ISMS.

- **Security Bulletins**: Regular bulletins or newsletters that update staff on recent security developments and reminders.

- ⚙️ **Dedicated Communication Platform**: Using an intranet site or a digital communication tool specifically for security matters.

Internal Hierarchy and Leadership in Communication:

- ⚙️ **Two-Way Communication Flow**: Ensure the communication hierarchy supports two-way feedback, allowing employees at all levels to raise security concerns or suggestions.

- ⚙️ **Leadership Engagement**: Encourage C-Level executives to actively communicate the importance of information security, making it a regular topic in larger company communications.

Incident Handling Communications:

- ⚙️ **Detailed Incident Response Plan**: Develop a comprehensive plan outlining the steps for incident reporting, incident roles, and internal and external communication protocols.

- ⚙️ **Regular Training and Drills**: Conduct regular training sessions and simulated drills to ensure employees are familiar with the incident response process.

Documenting Evidence of Awareness and Training:

- ⚙️ **Record Keeping**: Maintain records of all awareness and training activities, including attendance, feedback, and assessment results, to track effectiveness and for audit purposes.

Regular Updates and Adaptations:

- ⚙️ **Continuous Improvement**: Regularly review and update awareness and communication strategies to keep them relevant and effective, particularly in response to new security threats and organizational changes.

Communication of Security Awareness:

- ⬡ **Diverse Communication Methods**: Beyond traditional methods like email distribution, organizations should explore interactive ways to engage employees. This could include:

  - Interactive e-learning modules that cover key security topics.

  - Gamification of security training to make learning more engaging.

  - Integrating security discussions into regular team meetings.

- ⬡ **Role-Specific Awareness**: Communicate each employee's role in the ISMS, tailored to their specific responsibilities. This might include:

  - Developing security responsibility outlines within job descriptions.

  - Providing role-specific security training.

  - Including security-related objectives in performance evaluations.

External Communications

There are times when the organization needs to communicate with outside parties to maintain the ISMS. External communication is needed for vendors, business partners, regulatory bodies, and customers to align with the organization's information security policies and procedures. Here are some examples of external communications:

Compliance and Regulatory Reporting:

Communication with regulatory bodies is essential for compliance with legal and regulatory requirements. This includes reporting on compliance status, data breach notifications, and aligning with industry-specific security regulations.

Vendor and Third-Party Management:

Secure communication channels should be established with vendors and third parties, especially those who handle or have access to sensitive data. Vendor risk assessments, security requirements, and regular reviews of third-party security practices are important components of these communications.

Incident Response and Coordination:

In a security incident, timely and effective communication with external entities such as law enforcement, cybersecurity response teams, and affected parties is crucial. This involves reporting incidents, coordinating response efforts, and sharing information about threats and vulnerabilities.

Customer Trust and Transparency:

Communicating security measures and policies to customers can build trust and demonstrate the organization's commitment to protecting customer data. Transparency in data handling practices and privacy policies is also essential for customer relations.

Collaboration and Information Sharing:

Engaging in information-sharing initiatives with industry groups, security forums, and peer organizations helps to stay informed about emerging threats and best practices. Collaborative efforts in cybersecurity can improve overall security for the organization and the industry.

These are just some examples of external and internal communication. Keep in mind that every organization will have different needs.

Clause 7.5 Documented Information

The information security management system must be comprehensively documented. This documentation is crucial for ensuring continuity and consistency in implementing the ISMS. It serves as a reference that guides all workers in following established processes and policies.

Types of ISMS documents might include, but are not limited to:

- Security policy
- Supplier security agreements
- Asset inventories
- Disaster recovery plans
- Change management procedures
- Security procedures
- Risk assessments
- Incident response plans
- Audit reports
- Records of training and awareness activities

The Statement of Applicability is one of the most important documents of an ISMS. The SoA shows an organization's commitment to information security by detailing which controls have been implemented and providing justification for each decision.

7.5.1 Maintaining ISMS Documents

Managing and maintaining documents is essential for the effectiveness of the ISMS. These documents require the full backing of management and active support from subject matter experts familiar with the ISMS processes as they relate to the organization. Subject matter experts play a key role in creating, reviewing, and updating these documents to ensure they remain relevant and practical. Upper-level management must endorse and sign high-level policies to demonstrate their commitment and ensure alignment with organizational goals.

Required Documents (7.5.1a & 7.5.1b)

The organization is required to document its ISMS processes. They will tailor the documentation based on the size and nature of activities, processes, products, and services. Additionally, the complexity of its operations and the competence of its personnel should be considered. Essential documents supporting the ISMS's effectiveness include policies, objectives, risk assessment and treatment procedures, evidence of personnel competencies, and records of internal audits and management reviews. Effective control, timely review, and updates of these documents are important to ensure their continued relevance and applicability. Specific examples of critical documents include the ISMS Scope, Information Security Policy, Risk Assessment and Treatment Plan, Statement of Applicability, and records related to training and qualifications.

7.5.2 Creating and Updating ISMS Documents

Once the ISMS documents are created, they must be regularly reviewed and updated. The organization should determine the frequency of updates, considering factors like changes in IT infrastructure, business processes, legal requirements, and the external environment. The review process should include checking each document's description, format, and approvals. Significant changes should be tracked and communicated to relevant stakeholders. The organization will ensure update of the following:

- Each document has an Identification and Description. This might include a title, date, author, or reference number (7.5.2a).

- Consistent Formats Updated (e.g., language, software version, graphics) and media (e.g., paper, electronic) (7.5.2b).

- Review and approval for suitability and adequacy (7.5.2c)

7.5.3 Control of Documented Information

Control of documented information within the ISMS requires that the organization implements stringent measures to manage the distribution, access, modification, and storage of documentation. To ensure the integrity and confidentiality of ISMS documents, designated authorities within the organization are responsible for overseeing the following:

- Availability and suitability of documents for use, precisely where and when needed (7.5.2a).

- Protection against loss of confidentiality, unauthorized use, or compromise of integrity (7.5.2b).

- Procedures for the distribution, access, retrieval, and utilization of documents, ensuring secure and efficient handling (7.5.2c).

- Storage and preservation measures, including maintaining the legibility of documents (7.5.2d).

- Version control and management of document changes to maintain document integrity over time (7.5.2e).

⬡ Guidelines for the retention and proper disposition of documents, ensuring compliance with legal and regulatory requirements. (7.5.2f).

Each control process must be documented, outlining specific responsibilities and procedures to safeguard documented information against unauthorized access or misuse, thereby maintaining its confidentiality, integrity, and availability.

Regular Review and Auditing

It is critical to conduct regular reviews and audits of the ISMS documentation. This ensures that the documented information remains accurate, relevant, and effective in reflecting the organization's current security posture and compliance with relevant regulations and standards.

Clause 7 ISO 27001 Information Security Controls

Clause 7 provides support for the ISMS. Without the support of resources, the ISMS cannot be established.

Physical security controls are part of Clause 7. There can be no information security without good physical security. The ISO 27001:2002 has a list of these controls that align with Clause 7 (for more details, see Chapter 7, Annex A Informational Security Controls):

7.1 Physical security perimeters

7.2 Physical entry

7.3 Securing offices, rooms, and facilities

7.4 Physical security monitoring

7.5 Protecting against physical and environmental threats

7.6 Working in secure areas

7.7 Clear desk and clear screen

7.8 Equipment siting and protection

7.9 Security of assets off-premises

7.1 Storage media

7.11 Supporting utilities

7.12 Cabling security

7.13 Equipment maintenance

7.14 Secure disposal or re-use of equipment

7.5 Protecting against physical and environmental threats

7.6 Working in secure areas

7.7 Clear desk and clear screen

7.8 Equipment siting and protection

7.9 Security of assets off-premises

7.1 Storage media

7.11 Supporting utilities

7.12 Cabling security

7.13 Equipment maintenance

7.14 Secure disposal or re-use of equipment

Clause 8 Operation

After planning and supporting the information security management system, it is time to implement the controls selected in Clause 6. This clause gets in the weeds on the operation level where the work happens. Clause 8 covers:

- **8.1 Operational Planning and Control**: This involves establishing, implementing, and maintaining the processes needed to meet information security requirements. It includes managing changes in a controlled manner and ensuring consistent operation of the ISMS.

- **8.2 Information Security Risk Assessment**: This section details the process of conducting risk assessments consistent with the risk assessment process defined in Clause 6. This is a continual process and should be periodically reviewed.

⬡ **8.3 Information Security Risk Treatment**: This part involves implementing the risk treatment plan developed in Clause 6. It includes selecting and applying appropriate security controls from Annex A and integrating them into the organization's processes.

Clause 8.1 Operational Planning and Control

Once the organization has identified risks and requirements, it must figure out ways to implement security. These are methods (processes) that will be used throughout the organization.

The risk assessment process from Clause 6.1.2, Information Risk Assessment, plays a pivotal role here. It helps identify specific risks and determine the necessary actions and controls. Operational planning in Clause 8 directly ties these identified risks to specific operational actions and controls. For instance, if the risk assessment identifies data leakage as a high risk, operational controls might include implementing data encryption and access controls.

Examples of Operational Planning and Control:

- ⬡ Implementing robust access control measures to restrict unauthorized access to sensitive information.

- ⬡ Regular security audits to ensure ongoing compliance and to identify areas for improvement.

- ⬡ Encrypting sensitive data both in transit and at rest.

ISO 27002 and Annex A (listed here) cover the main operational needs. The organization pulls from ISO 27002 controls to select, implement, and manage controls based on the information security risk environment.

There are a few important things to do when conducting operational planning and control.

Documentation of Processes: Documenting each step of the operational process is crucial. This includes establishing criteria for successful implementation, outlining responsibilities, setting timelines, and maintaining records to ensure processes have been carried out as planned. See Clause 7.5 for examples of types of documents.

Review and Impact Assessment of Changes: Any changes in the operational processes should be rigorously reviewed. This review should assess the potential impacts of these changes on the organization's security posture and compliance status. The review team should include members from relevant departments, and the frequency of these reviews should align with the organization's risk management strategy.

Integration with Other ISO 27001 Clauses: Operational planning and control should align with the leadership responsibilities outlined in Clause 5 and feed into the performance evaluation in Clause 9. This ensures a cohesive approach to information security management throughout the organization.

Ensuring Continual Improvement: Monitoring and improving operational planning and control processes is essential. This includes regular reviews, adapting to changes in the risk landscape, and incorporating lessons learned from security incidents and audits. *More details on this in Clause 10.*

Implementing Controls Effectively: Controls should be implemented based on the organization's specific context. Tailoring these controls to fit the organization's operations' size, complexity, and nature is key to effective information security management.

Clause 8.2 Information Security Risk Assessment

Information security risk assessment is a crucial process that involves systematically and consistently assessing information security risks. This includes evaluating the potential impacts and likelihoods of these risks.

Detailed Risk Assessment Process:

- **Identify assets:** Determine what must be protected, considering physical and digital assets.

- **Evaluate threats and vulnerabilities:** Assess what could harm the assets and how these harms could occur.

- **Assess impact and likelihood:** Determine each identified risk's potential consequences and probability.

- **Determine risk levels:** Based on impact and likelihood, classify the level of risk (e.g., low, medium, high).

Linking with Operational Planning and Control (Clause 8.1):

- The outcomes of the risk assessment process should directly inform the operational planning and control measures. The identified risks should be addressed through specific operational controls to manage and mitigate them effectively.

Criteria for Risk Assessment (Reference to 6.1.2):

- The risk assessment should consider the criteria established in 6.1.2), such as the organization's risk tolerance, compliance requirements, and business objectives.

Frequency and Triggers for Risk Assessments:

- Conduct risk assessments regularly (e.g., annually) or when significant changes occur, such as new technology implementations, organizational restructuring, or major IT system upgrades.

Documenting and Reviewing Risk Assessment Outcomes:

- Retain documents of the risk assessment results.

- Regularly review and update these documents to ensure they accurately reflect the current risk landscape and any organizational changes.

Involvement of Relevant Stakeholders:

- To provide a comprehensive view of risks, engage relevant stakeholders in the risk assessment, including IT, HR, operations, and external parties like vendors or partners.

Risk Treatment Plan:

- Develop a risk treatment plan detailing how each identified risk will be treated (avoided, mitigated, transferred, or accepted), and document this plan.

Continual Improvement:

- Recognize that risk assessment is an ongoing activity. Regularly review and update the risk assessment process to adapt to new threats and organizational changes, ensuring continual improvement in the organization's information security posture.

Clause 8.3 Information Security Risk Treatment

This clause focuses on managing information security risks identified in the risk assessment process (Clause 8.2). It involves selecting appropriate risk treatment options and implementing risk treatment plans to address these risks effectively. There are a few key elements to keep in mind for risk treatment:

Selection of Risk Treatment Options:
Evaluate different treatment options for each identified risk. These options typically include risk avoidance, mitigation, transfer (e.g., through insurance), or acceptance (see Clause 6.1.3 in this writing for more details).

The selection should be based on factors such as the risk's severity, the organization's risk appetite, cost-benefit analysis, and compliance requirements.

Implementation of Risk Treatment Plans:
Develop detailed plans for each chosen risk treatment option. Plans should outline specific actions, responsible individuals, timelines, and required resources.

The plans should also consider potential impacts on business operations and ensure alignment with the organization's objectives and processes.

Integration with the Information Security Policy:
Ensure that risk treatment is effectively integrated within the information security policy. This includes aligning the treatment plans with the organization's information security policies and objectives.

Risk treatment actions should be incorporated into the ISMS's overall operational planning and control processes (Clause 8.1).

Monitoring and Review:
Regularly monitor the effectiveness of the implemented risk treatments. This includes tracking the progress of treatment actions and evaluating their impact on the risk levels. Review and update the risk treatment plans as necessary, especially after significant changes in the risk landscape or the organization.

Documentation and Record-Keeping:
Maintain comprehensive documentation of the risk treatment process. This includes records of the decision-making process for treatment options, details of the implemented plans, and monitoring reports.

Documentation provides evidence of compliance and supports continual improvement efforts within the ISMS.

Communication and Involvement of Stakeholders:
Effectively communicate the risk treatment plans and actions to relevant stakeholders, both internal and external. This ensures awareness and support for the risk treatment efforts. Involve key stakeholders in developing and reviewing risk treatment plans to leverage their insights and ensure comprehensive risk management.

Clause 8 ISO 27001 Information Security Controls

Clause 8 has ISO 27001 controls that align with it. These are technical security controls that support operations (for more details, see Chapter 7, Annex A Informational Security Controls):

8.1 User endpoint devices

8.2 Privileged access rights

8.3 Information access restriction

8.4 Access to source code

8.5 Secure authentication

8.6 Capacity management

8.7 Protection against malware

8.8 Management of technical vulnerabilities

8.9 Configuration management

8.10 Information deletion

8.11 Data masking

8.12 Data leakage prevention

8.13 Information backup

8.14 Redundancy of information processing facilities

8.15 Logging

8.16 Monitoring activities

8.17 Clock synchronization

8.18 Use of privileged utility programs

8.19 Installation of software on operational systems

8.20 Networks security

8.21 Security of network services

8.22 Segregation of networks

8.23 Web filtering

8.24 Use of cryptography

8.25 Secure development life cycle

8.26 Application security requirements

8.27 Secure system architecture and engineering principles

Chapter 5

CHECK – Monitoring and Evaluating the ISMS

Let me tell you something about evaluations. NOBODY... and I mean NOBODY wants to do a big certification or annual evaluation on systems. It's like the proctology, turn and cough, pap-smear of the cybersecurity world. You don't want to do it, but you must. The process is embarrassing. It feels humiliating to see your naked weaknesses found, pointed out, and put on display.

Don't get me wrong, everyone wants the positive results of the big evaluations (i.e., the certifications, a clean bill of health from professionals), but no one wants assessors to come in and tell them how and why their baby is ugly.

In this chapter, we talk about checking an organization's information security. Not all evaluations are stressful and evil. There are many less intrusive checks, and Clause 9 addresses why they must be done.

Once the ISMS is operational, it enters the 'Check' phase of the Plan-Do-Check-Act (PDCA) cycle. This phase is essential for assessing the system's security effectiveness and ensuring continuous improvement. It involves a thorough 'check' of the data produced by the ISMS, which includes monitoring, measuring, analyzing, and evaluating its performance. This is covered in Clause 9 of the ISO 27001 standard.

Clause 9 Performance Evaluation

A robust ISMS establishes mechanisms for detailed and actionable self-reflection on its processes and performance. Clause 9 delineates this critical evaluative process and is divided into the following key areas:

- 🔩 **9.1 Monitoring, Measurement, Analysis, and Evaluation**: This section outlines how to systematically monitor and measure the effectiveness of the ISMS, including analyzing and evaluating these findings to inform decision-making.

- 🔩 **9.2 Internal Audit**: This part focuses on the internal audit process, a crucial tool for independently assessing the ISMS's conformity to the organization's requirements and the standards set by ISO 27001.

- 🔩 **9.3 Management Review**: Here, the standard emphasizes the need for regular reviews by top management, ensuring that the ISMS remains suitable, adequate, and effective in changing internal and external factors.

By following these guidelines, an organization ensures that its ISMS complies with ISO 27001 and is practical and adaptable to evolving security needs and challenges.

Clause 9.1 Monitoring, Measurement, Analysis, and Evaluation

Clause 9.1 covers monitoring, measurement, analysis, and evaluation necessary to maintain and improve the ISMS. It covers the following considerations for an effective performance evaluation process.

Determining What to Monitor and Measure (9.1a)

What does the organization need to monitor and measure? This question is the first step to figuring out what parts of the information security system need to be checked and evaluated. This means looking at different security procedures and controls important for managing the security system. The goal is to fully understand how well the system works and find out what's working well and what needs improvement. Some examples of what needs to be monitored and measured in an ISMS, keeping security controls in mind:

- **Incident Response Time:** This involves tracking how quickly the security team responds to and handles security incidents, such as data breaches or cyber-attacks. A faster response time typically indicates a stronger security posture.

- **Compliance with Security Policies:** This means checking how well employees and systems follow the established security policies and guidelines. For example, ensuring that passwords are strong and changed regularly or that sensitive data is properly encrypted.

- **Network Traffic Anomalies:** Monitor data flow in and out of the network to detect unusual patterns or activities. This can help identify potential security threats, such as malware infections or unauthorized access attempts.

Methods for Monitoring, Measurement, Analysis, and Evaluation (9.1b)

Selecting appropriate ways to monitor, measure, analyze, and evaluate. These methods must be reliable, comparable, and reproducible. The validity of the results is essential for making informed decisions about the ISMS. For example, if the organization needs methods for measuring & monitoring Network Traffic Anomalies, they might select some or all of the following:

- ⚙ **Automated Network Monitoring Tools:** These tools continuously scan network traffic to detect unusual patterns or behaviors.

- ⚙ **Intrusion Detection Systems (IDS):** IDS are specialized tools designed to detect unauthorized access or anomalies in network traffic. They analyze network communications and compare them against a database of known threat signatures.

- ⚙ **Security Information Event Monitoring (SIEM):** These systems could assist in gathering all logs from network devices for cybersecurity analysis.

These tools and services require a solid, repeatable monitoring process by trained subject matter experts.

Scheduling Monitoring and Measuring Activities (9.1c)

The organization will determine the frequency and timing of monitoring and measuring activities. These should be conducted at intervals that provide meaningful data without causing undue disruption to normal operations. The organization might mandate weekly scans using automated network tools conducted by an information security scanning team or network engineering department.

Responsibility for Monitoring and Measurement (9.1d)

Assigning clear responsibilities for who will carry out these monitoring and measuring activities ensures accountability and consistency. The personnel chosen should have the necessary skills and knowledge to perform these tasks effectively.

The names of the personnel or units assigned don't matter as much as their duties. Here are some examples of roles or departments that might be responsible for monitoring and measuring network traffic anomalies:

- Vulnerability Management Team

- Network Management

- Risk Management Department

- Cybersecurity Specialist

- Information Security Office

Remember that network traffic anomalies are just one of many activities that might need to be monitored and measured for the ISMS.

Analysis and Evaluation of Results (9.1e)

Once the data is gathered, it is analyzed and evaluated. This analysis is essential for understanding the data's potential impact or implications and making informed decisions regarding the ISMS. Using our example of the network traffic anomaly, the analysis would allow the organization to determine if there is a security incident, such as a breach or misconfiguration, causing slower traffic or an error in the system.

Responsibility for Analysis and Evaluation (9.1f)

Determining who will analyze and evaluate the monitoring and measurement results is as important as the data collection itself. These individuals or teams should be able to interpret the data accurately and recommend actions based on the findings. The team conducting network traffic activity (mentioned in clause 9.1d) might differ from those tasked with analysis and evaluation. These personnel are typically skilled in data interpretation, risk assessment, incident handling, and decision-making. Here are examples of such roles:

- **Data Analysts:** Specialized in interpreting large sets of data, they can discern patterns and anomalies within the data collected by monitoring systems, aiding in understanding the security implications.

- **Security Analysts:** Focused on analyzing security threats and vulnerabilities, security analysts evaluate the severity and potential impact of identified anomalies or breaches.

- **Risk Assessment Team:** This team analyzes the data in the context of organizational risk,

- **IT Audit Team:** Responsible for evaluating the effectiveness of IT controls, the audit team uses the data to assess compliance with security policies and standards.

- **Incident Response Team:** While primarily responsible for managing security incidents, this team also evaluates incidents-related data to improve future response and prevention strategies.

- **Forensic Analysts:** In cases of security breaches, forensic analysts delve into the data to uncover the root cause and method of attack, providing crucial insights for evaluation.

Documentation and Evidence

All procedures and results from the monitoring, measurement, analysis, and evaluation processes must be documented. This documented information serves as evidence of the activities conducted and their outcomes. It is essential for auditing purposes and for demonstrating compliance with ISO 27001 standards.

Evaluating Information Security Performance and ISMS Effectiveness

The ultimate goal of these activities is to evaluate the overall performance of the information security initiatives and the effectiveness of the ISMS. This evaluation provides insights into how well the organization is managing its information security risks and whether the objectives of the ISMS are being achieved. Based on this evaluation, the organization can make informed decisions about necessary improvements or changes to the ISMS.

Clause 9.2 Internal Audit

It is sometimes called an internal assessment or self-assessment. The internal audit is used to help the organization check itself. This self-assessment will allow the organization to ensure that information security is on the right track, the controls remain effective, and the processes are being done. These are usually done more often than the larger annual, third-party, independent, compliance-type assessments. They are less stressful and have less at stake.

9.2.1 Internal Audit ISMS

Internal audits are a cornerstone of a good information security management system. These audits provide insights into both the compliance and the technical aspects of cybersecurity. ISO 27001:2022 mandates that organizations conduct these audits at planned intervals. The internal audit needs to have the following:

- **Conformance with Standards and Requirements (9.2.1a):** The organization creates the internal audit in accordance with its ISMS, and the ISMS will align with the requirements of ISO 27001:2022.

- **Effective Implementation and Maintenance (9.2.1b):** The audit evaluates whether the ISMS is effectively implemented and consistently maintained over time, ensuring its continued relevance and efficiency.

9.2.2 *Internal Audit Program*

For internal auditing to be consistent and effective, it must be supported by an internal audit program. This program should encompass the following elements:

- **Planning and Frequency**: The frequency of the audits should be determined based on various factors, such as the significance of the processes involved and the outcomes of previous audits.

- **Audit Methodology**: The audit methods should be defined clearly, encompassing all necessary steps from initiation to conclusion.

- **Responsibilities and Requirements**: Clear responsibilities should be assigned for the planning and execution of the audits.

- **Audit Criteria and Scope Definition (9.2.2a)**: Specific criteria and scope must be established for each audit. This helps focus the audit on the most pertinent aspects of the ISMS.

- **Selection of Auditors (9.2.2b)**: Auditors should be chosen based on their objectivity and impartiality.

- **Reporting (9.2.2c)**: The findings of the audits must be effectively communicated to relevant management.

- **Documentation and Evidence**: Documented evidence of the audit program's implementation and the results of the audits must be maintained. This serves as proof of compliance and a record for future reference.

Internal auditing is a vital process in assessing the health and effectiveness of ISMS. It helps organizations identify areas for improvement and reassures stakeholders that information security is being managed diligently.

Clause 9.3 Management Review

Clause 9.3 of ISO 27001:2022 concerns the organization's planned periodic ISMS. This is so that it keeps up to date and maintains its relevance, adequacy, and effectiveness.

9.3.1 ISMS Management Review

The management review is a critical component of the information security management system. It mandates that top management periodically review the ISMS to ensure its ongoing relevance, adequacy, and effectiveness in changing external and internal factors.

9.3.2 Management Review Inputs

A comprehensive management review should encompass various aspects crucial for the ISMS's effective functioning. These aspects include:

Review of Past Actions (9.3.2a): Evaluating the status of actions decided upon in previous management reviews, checking their completion and effectiveness.

External and Internal Changes (9.3.2b): Assessing how changes in external and internal contexts affect the ISMS. This includes regulatory, technological, and organizational changes.

Needs and Expectations of Interested Parties (9.3.2c): Considering any changes in the needs and expectations of stakeholders that are relevant to the ISMS.

Information Security Performance Feedback (9.3.2d): Analyzing various metrics and feedback to gauge the ISMS's performance. This includes:

- Nonconformities and corrective actions taken.
- Results from monitoring and measurement activities.
- Outcomes of internal and external audits.
- Achievement of information security objectives.

Stakeholder Feedback (9.3.2e): Incorporating feedback from interested parties may provide insights into areas needing attention or improvement.

Risk Assessment and Risk Treatment Plan (9.3.2f): Review the results of the latest risk assessments and the progress of the risk treatment plan to ensure continued risk management effectiveness.

Opportunities for Continual Improvement (9.3.2g): Identifying potential areas for improvement in the ISMS.

9.3.3 Management Review Results

The outcome of the management review should be action-oriented and forward-looking. It must include:

- **Decisions on Continual Improvement**: Identifying and deciding upon opportunities for enhancing the ISMS.
- **Needs for Changes to the ISMS**: Determining if aspects of the ISMS require modification better to meet the organization's information security needs and objectives.

This management review process ensures the ISMS remains dynamic and responsive to the ever-evolving information security landscape. It assists top management in making informed decisions that uphold the robustness and effectiveness of the ISMS, ensuring that it continues to align with the organization's overall strategic direction and objectives.

Chapter 6

ACT – Keep Improving the ISMS

"We all need people who will give us feedback. That's how we improve."

– Bill Gates.

In the PDCA, the ACT stage is pivotal. It's not just the final step but a critical phase where the organization reflects on the assessments and reviews conducted in the CHECK stage to enhance its ISMS.

Clause 10 Improvement

Clause 10 of ISO 27001:2022 focuses on the ongoing improvements of the ISMS. This is important to maintaining and elevating the performance of information security. Here are the principles outlined in this chapter:

- 10.1 Continual Improvement
- 10.2 Nonconformity and Corrective Action

Clause 10.1 Continual improvement

This clause requires a strategic approach to refining all key aspects of the ISMS, focusing on confidentiality, integrity, availability, and the processes that uphold them. These enhancements should be grounded in regular evaluations and feedback, ensuring the ISMS remains robust and responsive to evolving security challenges and regulatory requirements. Continual improvement serves several critical functions:

- **Relevance Maintenance:** This ensures the ISMS adapts to the changing threat landscape, maintaining its relevance.

- **Gap Identification and Resolution:** Continuous evaluation helps identify and address previously unnoticed vulnerabilities.

- **Control Optimization:** Regular reviews facilitate fine-tuning existing controls for optimal performance.

- ⚙ **Regulatory Compliance:** This process aids in maintaining compliance with ISO 27001 standards and other industry-specific regulations.

- ⚙ **Documentation and Evidence:** Continual improvement processes provide documented proof of ongoing efforts to strengthen and sustain the ISMS.

Clause 10.2 Nonconformity and Corrective Action

A nonconformity happens when a requirement stated in the ISMS is not met. It can be due to a missed opportunity, a lack of proper planning, not implementing controls, or other reasons. Non-conformities can be of several types:

- ⚙ Failure to fulfil a requirement in the ISMS.

- ⚙ Lack of proper implementation of an ISMS requirement.

- ⚙ Failure to comply properly with legal, contractual, or customer requirements.

Some common reasons the above types of non-conformities can occur are:

- ⚙ Responsible persons not behaving as expected by procedures and policies.

- ⚙ Suppliers not providing agreed-upon products or services.

- ⚙ Projects not delivering expected outcomes, either because of delay or improper execution.

- ⚙ Controls not operating as intended due to misconfiguration or tool limitations.

It is important to note that in the event of a security incident, it is safe to assume that a nonconformity is occurring somewhere. Still, nonconformity can occur even when there aren't any security incidents.

How to Apply Corrective Actions? (10.2a)

We should have pre-defined processes for handling nonconformity, and in the event of a nonconformity, we should follow the steps outlined to fix it. The corrective process should include:

- Identifying the extent and impact of the nonconformity.

- Performing appropriate actions to contain the impact of the non-conformity, either by switching to a previous state or any other appropriate state of the control

- Communicating with relevant personnel to ensure that corrections are carried out.

- Carrying out corrective actions.

- Monitoring and following up on the corrective actions ensure the intended result is achieved.

- Communicating with other relevant interested parties and stakeholders as appropriate.

Evaluate the Need for Corrective Action (10.2b)

Not all nonconformities need correction or can be corrected. Various practical constraints include budgets, risk treatment, and resource availability. A few other things must be considered when identifying a nonconformity and applying corrective actions.

Based on the impact, repetitiveness, and other established criteria, the organization needs to decide if corrective action is necessary. Leadership will need to ensure that the nonconformity is reviewed. They must also consider similar situations to detect patterns that point to a root cause.

Implementing Corrective Actions (10.2c)

Implementing corrective actions according to the plan is critical in addressing nonconformities. These actions must be executed as outlined in the planned response. This ensures a targeted approach to specific issues, considering the unique requirements of the identified non-conformities.

Examples of corrective action might include:

- **Security Breach**: The planned action might involve strengthening firewalls and training staff on new security protocols if a security breach is identified.

- **Data Loss Incident**: In case of data loss, the action plan could include implementing more robust data backup procedures and reviewing access controls.

- **Compliance Issue**: Corrective actions may involve revising policies and conducting additional staff training on regulatory requirements for a compliance-related nonconformity.

Reviewing Effectiveness of Corrective Actions (10.2d)

Once corrective actions are implemented, a thorough review of their effectiveness is crucial. This review involves comparing the actual outcomes with the expected results, thereby evaluating whether the corrective actions have successfully resolved the issues. This step is vital to ensure the appropriateness of the actions taken.

Examples of reviewing effectiveness:

- ⚙ **Security Breach Example**:

    - After implementing stronger security protocols, review the frequency and severity of new breaches.

    - Assess the time taken to detect and respond to breaches compared to before the corrective actions.

- ⚙ **Data Loss Incident Example**:

    - After implementing improved data backup procedures, evaluate the recovery success rate in case of data loss incidents.

    - Analyze the time required to restore data and any residual impact on operations.

- ⚙ **Compliance Issue Example**:

    - Following policy revisions to address compliance gaps, conduct an internal audit to ensure all areas meet regulatory standards.

    - Review employee understanding and adherence to these new policies through surveys or interviews.

Making Changes to the ISMS (10.2e)

Based on the outcomes and learnings from the corrective actions, changes to the Information Security Management System may be necessary. This step is about updating and refining the ISMS to incorporate the insights gained, ensuring the system is robust and resilient against future occurrences of similar nonconformities.

Documenting Nonconformities and Actions (10.2f & 10.2g)

Documenting the nature of nonconformities and subsequent actions taken, along with the results of these corrective actions, is an essential aspect of Clause 10.2. This documentation is crucial evidence of the ISMS's maintenance and continual improvement efforts, providing valuable records for audits, reviews, and ongoing system management.

Each step underlines the importance of a proactive and methodical approach to managing and improving the ISMS, ensuring its effectiveness and alignment with ISO 27001:2022 standards.

Chapter 7

Annex A Information Security Controls

I wish I could say something funny about not having security controls, but its actually shocking to see the same banks, healthcare, and government organizations we rely on without the controls implemented effectively.

An effective information security management system is a process that applies security controls to protect the confidentiality, integrity, and availability of data.

ISO 27001:2022 has Annex A, which lists 93 information security controls. These controls come from ISO 27002:2022 and align with Clauses 5 to 8 of 27001. These controls are referenced in Clause 6.1.3, Information Security Risk Treatment.

There are 4 sets of ISMS controls:

- Organizational Controls
- People Controls
- Physical Controls
- Technological Controls

5.0 Organizational Controls

37 Organizational controls lay the foundation for the ISMS by defining processes, procedures, policies, and other elements that guide an organization's mission and operations. These controls ensure that information security is integrated into the organizational fabric, with transparent management directives, defined roles and responsibilities, and established processes for handling information securely. These are aligned with Clause 5 of the ISO 27001.

5.1 Information Security Policy Framework

Establish a comprehensive set of security policies tailored to the organization's needs. These should be formally approved by management, widely distributed, acknowledged by staff and stakeholders, and regularly reviewed for relevance and effectiveness, especially after significant organizational changes.

5.2 Allocation of Information Security Responsibilities

Clearly define and assign specific information security roles and duties within the organization to ensure that all employees understand their responsibilities in maintaining and enforcing security measures in line with organizational needs.

5.3 Segregation of Duties

Separate roles and responsibilities that could potentially conflict to reduce the risk of unauthorized or unintentional modification or misuse of the organization's information assets. This control aims to prevent fraud and errors by dispersing the tasks and associated privileges for critical processes.

5.4 Managerial Information Security Oversight

Management must enforce compliance with the organization's information security policies and procedures across all levels of personnel, ensuring that everyone contributes to the organization's security posture.

5.5 Contact with Authorities

Establish and sustain communication with law enforcement and regulatory bodies to ensure the organization remains aligned with legal requirements and can respond swiftly to legal or regulatory actions related to information security.

5.6 Engagement with Special Interest Groups

Maintain active relationships with special interest groups, security forums, and professional associations to share knowledge, stay updated on the latest security trends, and collaborate on best practices.

5.7 Threat Intelligence Gathering

Proactively collect and analyze data on potential information security threats to produce actionable intelligence to inform the organization's security strategies and defences.

5.8 Secure Project Management

Integrate information security measures into all project management processes to ensure that projects are executed with security considerations from start to finish.

5.9 Asset Inventory Management

Develop and regularly update an inventory of all information and associated assets, including their ownership, to manage them effectively and securely.

5.10 Acceptable Use Policy Implementation

Define and enforce guidelines for the acceptable use of information and associated assets to prevent misuse and ensure all users handle organizational assets responsibly.

5.11 Asset Return Procedures

Ensure clear procedures are in place to return organizational assets when individuals leave or end their contract or agreement.

5.12 Information Classification Protocol

Classify information based on its security requirements, such as confidentiality, integrity, and availability, to apply appropriate safeguards and access controls.

5.13 Information Labelling

Control procedures to ensure that information is labelled in line with the organization's classification policy.

5.14 Secure Information Transfer

Procedures to govern the secure transfer of information within the organization and with external parties.

5.15 Robust Access Control

Establishment of controls to manage physical and logical access to information based on business needs and security requirements.

5.16 Comprehensive Identity Management

Lifecycle management of user identities to ensure appropriate access and security across the organization.

5.17 Authentication Management

Controlled allocation and management of authentication mechanisms, ensuring proper handling and security of authentication data.

5.18 Managed Access Rights

Provision, review, and adjustment of access rights in accordance with organizational access control policies.

5.19 Supplier Relationship Security

Defining and implementing processes to manage risks related to supplier relationships and their impact on information security.

5.20 Security in Supplier Agreements

Information security requirements should be included in agreements with suppliers to address associated risks.

5.21 ICT Supply Chain Security

Management of information security risks throughout the information and communication technology (ICT) supply chain.

5.22 Supplier Service Change Management

Regular monitoring and management of changes in supplier security practices and service delivery.

5.23 Cloud Services Security

Establishment of processes for secure use and management of cloud services.

5.24 Incident Management Preparedness

Planning and preparation for effective information security incident management.

5.25 Security Event Assessment

Evaluation of information security events to determine if they constitute security incidents.

5.26 Incident Response

Addressing information security incidents in accordance with documented procedures.

5.27 Incident Knowledge Application

Utilization of lessons learned from information security incidents to strengthen controls.

5.28 Evidence Collection

Establishment of processes for evidence collection related to information security events.

5.29 Security During Disruptions

Planning for the maintenance of information security during organizational disruptions.

5.30 ICT Continuity for Business

Preparation and testing of ICT readiness to support business continuity objectives.

5.31 Compliance with Legal Requirements

Identification and documentation of legal and contractual information security requirements.

5.32 Intellectual Property Protection

Implementation of measures to protect intellectual property rights.

5.33 Record Protection

Safeguarding records from loss, destruction, and unauthorized access or disclosure.

5.34 Privacy and PII Protection

Ensuring privacy and protection of personally identifiable information in line with legal and regulatory requirements.

5.35 Independent Security Review

Periodic independent review of the organization's information security management practices.

5.36 Policy and Standard Compliance

Regular review to ensure compliance with information security policies and standards.

5.37 Documented Operating Procedures

Establishing, maintaining, and making documented procedures for operating information processing facilities readily available.

6.0 People Controls

There are 8 people-based security controls that assist with the planning phase of Clause 6. It's people that make the ISMS happen. The "people controls" include personnel screening, education, and working conditions. These are aligned with Clause 6 of 27001.

6.1 Rigorous Personnel Screening

Conducting background checks and ongoing verification for all personnel in alignment with legal and ethical standards.

6.2 Defined Employment Conditions

Specification of information security responsibilities within employment contracts.

6.3 Security Awareness Training

Provision of information security awareness and training to all relevant personnel.

6.4 Disciplinary Measures

Establishment of a formal process for disciplinary actions against policy violations.

6.5 Post-Employment Responsibilities

Definition and communication of information security duties that persist beyond employment termination.

6.6 Confidentiality Agreements

Create and maintain confidentiality or non-disclosure agreements to protect sensitive information.

6.7 Secure Remote Working

Implementation of security measures for remote working scenarios.

6.8 Event Reporting Mechanism

Provision of channels for personnel to report suspected information security events.

7.0 Physical Controls

There are 14 physical and environmental controls that align with Clause 7. Physical security protects the information systems and the people in the organization following the processes and procedures.

7.1 Physical Security Perimeters

Definition and protection of physical perimeters around sensitive information areas.

7.2 Controlled Physical Access

Regulation of access to secure areas through appropriate controls.

7.3 Office and Facility Security

Design and application of physical security for organizational premises.

7.4 Continuous Physical Monitoring

Ongoing surveillance to prevent unauthorized access to facilities.

7.5 Environmental Threat Protection

Measures to guard against physical and environmental threats.

7.6 Secured Area Protocols

Security protocols specifically for working within secured areas.

7.7 Clean Desk and Screen Policy

Policies for maintaining clear desks and screens to protect sensitive information.

7.8 Secure Equipment Placement

Strategic siting and protection of equipment to prevent unauthorized access.

7.9 Off-Premises Asset Security

Protection measures for assets located outside the organization's premises.

7.10 Storage Media Lifecycle Management

Managing storage media from acquisition to disposal aligns with data handling requirements.

7.11 Utility Failure Safeguards

Protection of information processing facilities from utility failures.

7.12 Cabling Security

Implement protective measures for cabling to prevent damage, interception, or interference that could compromise the power, data, and support services.

7.13 Equipment Maintenance

Ensure regular and correct equipment maintenance to maintain its availability, integrity, and the confidentiality of the information it processes or stores.

7.14 Secure Disposal or Re-Use of Equipment

Confirm that sensitive data and licensed software are securely removed or overwritten before the disposal or re-use of storage-containing equipment.

8.0 Technological Controls

34 technical controls install, configure, or update the applicable security features of the information system. The controls apply to the systems required for the essential functions of the organization's operations, such as business and mission. Workstations, servers, and network devices need technical security to comply with the ISMS.

8.1 Endpoint Device Security

Ensure that information stored on or accessed through endpoint devices, such as desktops, laptops, and smartphones, is adequately secured against unauthorized access and breaches.

8.2 Management of Privileged Access

Privileged access rights should be carefully allocated, monitored, and managed to prevent abuse of elevated permissions, which could lead to security incidents.

8.3 Restricting Information Access

Access to information and associated assets must be restricted and controlled based on the organization's specific policies.

8.4 Source Code Access Management

Access to source code and development tools should be tightly managed to protect intellectual property and prevent unauthorized changes.

8.5 Implementation of Secure Authentication

Implement strong authentication mechanisms to verify the identity of users and secure access to systems in line with access control policies.

8.6 Resource Capacity Management

Monitor and manage resource utilization to ensure the IT infrastructure meets current and future workload demands effectively.

8.7 Malware Protection

Deploy anti-malware solutions and conduct user training to prevent, detect, and respond to malicious software threats.

8.8 Handling Technical Vulnerabilities

Stay informed about technical vulnerabilities affecting systems in use; evaluate risks and apply necessary measures to mitigate exposure.

8.9 System Configuration Management

Establish and maintain secure configurations for IT systems and networks, documenting and regularly reviewing settings to ensure ongoing security.

8.10 Secure Information Deletion

Ensure that data is securely deleted from all systems and storage media when it is no longer required to prevent unauthorized access or recovery.

8.11 Data Masking Strategies

Utilize data masking techniques in line with access control policies to protect sensitive information from exposure, especially in environments where data is used for testing or analytics.

8.12 Data Leakage Prevention

Apply measures across systems and networks to prevent unauthorized disclosure of sensitive information, ensuring that data leakage risks are mitigated.

8.13 Robust Information Backup

Maintain and regularly test backup copies of critical information and systems, ensuring data can be recovered in the event of a loss or failure.

8.14 Ensuring Redundancy of Systems

Implement redundant information processing facilities to provide continuity of service and data availability in case of system failure.

8.15 Activity Logging

Produce and maintain logs for all system activities, exceptions, and security events to support incident detection and forensic analysis.

8.16 System and Network Monitoring

Continuously monitor for irregular activities within networks, systems, and applications, and respond swiftly to any potential security threats.

8.17 Time Synchronization

Synchronize all system clocks within the information processing infrastructure to a standardized time source for accuracy and consistency.

8.18 Controlled Use of Utility Programs

Regulate the use of system utilities capable of overriding controls to prevent misuse and protect system integrity.

8.19 Controlled Software Installations

Implement secure processes for installing software on operational systems to prevent unauthorized or harmful software deployment.

8.20 Comprehensive Network Security

Secure networks and network devices to safeguard information assets from unauthorized access, modifications, or destruction.

8.21 Network Services Security

Network services should have defined security mechanisms, service levels, and requirements regularly identified, implemented, and monitored to ensure security and reliability.

8.22 Network Segregation

Segregate networks to separate various types of information services, user groups, and information systems, enhancing security and reducing the risk of cross-contamination.

8.23 Web Content Filtering

Access to external websites by implementing web filtering to minimize the risk of exposure to malicious software and inappropriate content.

8.24 Cryptography Implementation

Establish and follow strict rules for using cryptography, including managing cryptographic keys, to ensure secure storage and transmission of sensitive information.

8.25 Secure Software Development Lifecycle

Apply a secure development lifecycle to software and systems to ensure security is considered and integrated at each stage of development.

8.26 Defining Application Security Requirements

Identify and document security requirements for new applications during the development or acquisition phase to ensure they meet organizational security standards.

8.27 Secure System Architecture

Adopt and maintain secure engineering principles for system architecture to ensure robust security from the ground up in system development.

8.28 Principles of Secure Coding

Apply secure coding practices to software development to prevent vulnerabilities and enhance the security of applications.

8.29 Security Testing in Software Development

Integrate security testing into the development and acceptance processes to identify and mitigate potential security issues before deployment.

8.30 Management of Outsourced Development

Oversee and review outsourced development projects to ensure external teams adhere to the organization's security standards and practices.

8.31 Environment Isolation

Keep development, testing, and production environments separate and secure to prevent unauthorized access and potential breaches.

8.32 Change Management Procedures

Implement change management practices for information systems to control and document any changes, reducing the risk of unintended service disruptions or security breaches.

8.33 Management of Test Data

Ensure that test information is carefully chosen, protected, and handled, maintaining the integrity and security of the data used in testing environments.

8.34 Safeguarding Systems During Audits

Protect information systems during audit tests and other activities by planning and coordinating with the relevant management to minimize operational risks.

Chapter 8

27001, 27002, and 27005

The ISO 27001:2022 standard is a cornerstone for establishing a robust information security management system, offering organizations a comprehensive framework for safeguarding information assets. However, implementing an ISMS is a multifaceted endeavor that requires additional guidance. This is where the broader ISO 27000 series of standards comes in!

In particular, ISO 27002:2022 and ISO 27005 complement ISO 27001 by offering detailed insights into effective control implementation and risk management strategies.

ISO 27002:2022 is an indispensable companion to ISO 27001, expanding on the controls listed in Annex A of ISO 27001. It serves as an exhaustive catalog that lists these controls and provides granular detail on the practical aspects of their implementation. Organizations can turn to ISO 27002 for nuanced explanations of each control's intent, the expected outcomes, and guidance on implementing these controls. The standard illuminates the path from the theoretical underpinnings of ISO 27001 to the tangible steps required to achieve its security objectives.

Where ISO 27002 offers the 'what' and 'how' of a control application, ISO 27005 delves into the 'why' by focusing on information security risk management. It provides a structured and systematic approach to risk assessment—a fundamental aspect of any ISMS. ISO 27005 guides organizations through identifying potential security threats, quantifying the associated risks, and determining the appropriate management response. By aligning risk management processes with the controls outlined in ISO 27002, organizations can ensure a balanced and informed approach to mitigating risk.

The synergy between ISO 27001, 27002, and 27005 creates a comprehensive organizational blueprint. ISO 27001 sets the strategic framework, ISO 27002 details the tactical control implementations, and ISO 27005 provides the operational procedures for assessing and managing risks. Together, they form a triad that equips organizations with the knowledge and tools necessary for a dynamic and effective ISMS capable of responding to an ever-evolving risk landscape.

In pursuing robust information security, organizations should not view ISO 27001 in isolation but should harness the collective wisdom of the 27000 families. Embracing the full suite of guidance can transform an organization's security posture from reactive to proactive, ensuring compliance and resilience against the backdrop of a challenging digital ecosystem. With the ISO 27000 series as a guide, organizations can confidently navigate the complexities of information security, knowing they have a world-class framework to support their journey toward securing their most valuable information assets.

The Evolution of ISO 27001

To truly understand the purpose of ISO 27001, looking at how it came to be and how it has evolved over the years can be helpful.

In the early 1990s, the UK government's Department of Trade and Industry (DTI) felt the need for a set of criteria to evaluate the security of IT security products. They asked the Commercial Computer Security Center (CCSC) for help. Along with this,

CCSC was also asked to create a standard for security best practices. This document created by the CCSC was known as DISC PD003. Work on DISC PD003 continued and evolved into two major parts: BS7799-1 and BS7799-2.

BS7799-1 was later divided into 10 parts, which laid the groundwork for ISO 27002. BS7799-2 evolved into a formal standard for developing an ISMS. First published in 1998 by the British Standards Institution (BSI), this document eventually evolved into ISO 27001 in October 2005.

It was revised in 2013 in response to changes in the security landscape and to improve the standard and its processes. The following notable updates were made:

- Large organizations could continue using any continual improvement process they currently use (the Plan-Do-Check-Act process was no longer required).

- Entry barriers for organizations required to use specific process models were reduced.

- The standard became more flexible in general.

- Terms and definitions were standardized across the ISO 27000 family, using those provided in ISO 27000:2012.

- The standard was linked to ISO 31000 risk assessment, which tied together information security risk management and corporate risk management approaches.

There were also comparatively minor but notable updates to the standard in 2017. The core requirements remained the same, with only minor adjustments, such as the addition of 'EN' to the title and incorporation of the 2017 date. These changes primarily indicated the European Body's added approval of this standard.

The latest updates to the standard were made in 2022. This did not change the body of the standard, but the security controls listed in ISO 27001 were updated.

- The controls were also categorized into more useful groups, enabling streamlining as they are now organized into 4 sections (instead of 14) with 93 controls (instead of 114). The four new sections are Organizational Controls, People Controls, Physical Controls, and Technological Controls.

- 23 of the controls were renamed to make them easier to understand. No controls were deleted, but 57 controls were merged into 24.

- One control was split into the 18.2.3 Technical Compliance Review. This was split into 5.36 Conformance with Policies, rules, and Standards for Information Security and 8.8 Management of Technical Vulnerabilities

- In addition to the split control, 11 new controls were added. These are:

  - *5.7* Threat Intelligence

  - 5.23 Information security for the use of cloud services

  - 5.30 ICT readiness for business continuity

  - 7.4 Physical security monitoring

  - 8.10 Information deletion

  - 8.11 Data masking

  - 8.12 Data leakage prevention

  - 8.16 Monitoring activities

  - 8.23 Web filtering

  - 8.28 Secure coding.

Speaking from personal experience, ISO 27001 is one of the best standards an organization can use. The combination of all the clauses provides what every medium and large organization needs to protect the confidentiality, integrity, and availability of important data. Its vendor and industry-neutral and is highly regarded all over the world. Related frameworks, standards, and laws (such as HIPAA, NIST 800, and GDRP) are huge but only in a given country or industry.

As a cybersecurity professional, understanding the ISO 27001 standard and how it relates to the security controls detailed in ISO 27002 is crucial because it opens the door to understanding other frameworks and governance, risk, and compliance as a whole.

References

Alvaro (2023, November 2). *10 Common ISO 27001 Challenges in Achieving Compliance*. Compleye.io. https://compleye.io/articles/10-common-ISO 27001-challenges-in-achieving-compliance/

Anwita. (2023, October 1). *What is ISO 27003? [Complete Section Wise Breakdown]*. Sprinto. https://sprinto.com/blog/ISO27003-guide/#:~:text=ISO%2027003%20is%20a%20set

CFO (2023, June 5). *The CFO Survey*. cfosurvey.org. https://www.richmondfed.org/cfosurvey/

Chin, K. (2023, August 3). *What is an ISMS (Information Security Management System)? | UpGuard*. www.upguard.com. https://www.upguard.com/blog/isms

Comparing ISO Protect • Comply • Thrive. (2700). https://www.itgovernance.co.uk/download/27001-update-reference-sheet.pdf

Cook, L. (2022, July 22). *The Evolution of ISO 27001*. CYJAX. https://www.cyjax.com/the-evolution-of-ISO 27001/

Cybersecurity Risk Assessment | IT Governance USA. (n.d.). Itgovernanceusa.com. https://www.itgovernanceusa.com/cyber-security-risk-assessments#:~:text=A%20cybersecurity%20risk%20assessment%20is

Das, D. (2023, August 13). *ISO 27003 - ISO 27001's true companion*. Www.linkedin.com.

https://www.linkedin.com/pulse/ISO27003-27001s-true-companion-dipen-das-cisa-cissp

Dunham, R. (2018, July 26). *Information Security Policies: Why They Are Important to Your Organization.* Linford & Company LLP. https://linfordco.com/blog/information-security-policies/

Dutton, J. (2018, July 27). *What exactly is an information security management system (ISMS)? - IT Governance USA Blog.* IT Governance USA Blog. https://www.itgovernanceusa.com/blog/what-exactly-is-an-information-security-management-system-isms-2

Gracy, M. (2023a, March 25). *Top 7 Benefits of ISMS Implementation in 2023.* Sprinto. https://sprinto.com/blog/benefits-of-implementing-isms/

Gracy, M. (2023b, October 17). *ISO/IEC 27002:2022 Security Controls [Newly Updated Guide].* Sprinto. https://sprinto.com/blog/ISO27002-controls/#:~:text=ISO%2027002%20provides%20comprehensive%20guidance

Hanna, K. T. (2023). *What is ISO 27001? - Definition from WhatIs.com.* WhatIs.com. https://www.techtarget.com/whatis/definition/ISO27001

Information security, cybersecurity and privacy protection - Information security management systems - Requirements. (2022). http://www.itref.ir/uploads/editor/2ef522.pdf

Information Security Management System (ISMS) | Myra. (2023, January 17). Www.myrasecurity.com. https://www.myrasecurity.com/en/knowledge-hub/information-security-management-system-isms/

Information technology -Security techniques -Information security management systems -Guidance. (n.d.). https://www.amnafzar.net/files/1/ISO%2027000/ISO%20IEC%2027003-2017.pdf

Information technology — Security techniques — Information security management — Monitoring, measurement, analysis and evaluation. (n.d.). International Standard. https://www.amnafzar.net/files/1/ISO%2027000/ISO%20IEC%2027004-2016.pdf

Irwin, L. (2019, April 18). *ISO 27001 checklist: a step-by-step guide to implementation - IT Governance UK Blog.* IT Governance UK Blog. https://www.itgovernance.co.uk/blog/ISO27001-checklist-a-step-by-step-guide-to-implementation

ISACA. (2011, July 1). *2011 Planning for and Implementing ISO 27001.* Www.isaca.org. https://www.isaca.org/resources/isaca-journal/past-issues/2011/2011-planning-for-and-implementing-ISO 27001

ISMS – Information Security Management System. (n.d.). OTRS. https://otrs.com/use-cases/isms/

ISMS documentation. (n.d.). Www.iso27001security.com. https://www.iso27001security.com/html/documentation.html

isms.online. (2020, December 7). *ISO 27002: The Code of Practice for Information Security Controls.* ISMS.online. https://www.isms.online/ISO 27002/

ISO 27001: 2022 - Key Changes and Approaches to Transition | Protiviti United States. (n.d.). Www.protiviti.com. Retrieved December 15, 2023, from https://www.protiviti.com/us-en/whitepaper/ISO27001-2022-key-changes-and-approaches-transition

ISO 27001:2022 GAP GUIDE. (n.d.). IQA. Retrieved December 15, 2023, from https://www.nqa.com/getmedia/94f5e5cb-2cbe-4c97-9a3f-fe0d4ed3e0a2/Final-27001-Gap-Guide-Update-June-23.pdf

ISO 27002: Security Controls. (2016). Itgovernanceusa.com https://www.itgovernanceusa.com/iso27002

ISO 27003: Guidance for ISO 27001 Implementation. (2020, December 7). ISMS.online. https://www.isms.online/ISO 27003/

ISO 27003: Information Security Techniques for ISMS - DataGuard. (n.d.). Www.dataguard.co.uk. https://www.dataguard.co.uk/blog/ISO 27003/

ITGovernance. (2016). *ISO 27001 Benefits | IT Governance UK.* Itgovernance.co.uk. https://www.itgovernance.co.uk/iso27001-benefits

kaur, J., Kocchar, T. S., Ganguli, S., & Rajest, S. (2021, March). *Evolution of Management System Certification: An overview.* Research Gate. http://dx.doi.org/10.46532/978-81-950008-7-6_008

Kosutic, D. (2016, May 23). *What is an ISMS – ISO 27001 Information Security Management System.* Advisera.com. https://advisera.com/27001academy/blog/2016/05/23/information-security-management-system-isms-according-ISO 27001/

Leal, R. (2017, April 10). *ISO 27001 resources: How to evidence their availability in an ISMS.* Advisera.com. https://advisera.com/27001academy/blog/2017/04/10/how-to-demonstrate-resource-provision-in-ISO 27001/

Magnusson, A. (2023, March 23). *ISO 27001 vs. 27002 vs. 27003: Understanding the Difference | strongDM*. Discover.strongdm.com. https://www.strongdm.com/blog/ISO 27001-vs-27002-vs-27003

Nahar, N. (2021, September 22). *10 Importance of Information Security Audit*. ZEVENET. https://www.zevenet.com/blog/10-importance-of-information-security-audit/

Talia. (2023, February 9). *5 Key Benefits of ISO 27001 Certification*. Scytale. https://scytale.ai/resources/benefits-of-ISO 27001-certification/

The Benefits of Implementing an Information Security Management System (ISMS) Ireland. (2016). Itgovernance.eu. https://www.itgovernance.eu/en-ie/isms-benefits-ie

The Different Between ISO 27001:2013 & ISO 27001:2017 - QCS. (2019, July 8). OCS International. https://qcsl.co.uk/whats-the-difference-between-ISO 270012013-and-iso270012017

The History of ISO 27001. (n.d.). Secureframe. https://secureframe.com/hub/ISO27001/history

The new ISO/IEC 27001:2022 standard. (n.d.). Www.bsigroup.com. https://www.bsigroup.com/en-US/ISO IEC-27001-Information-Security/2022-revision/

Title of the brochure or column title. (n.d.). https://kpmg.com/kpmg-us/content/dam/kpmg/pdf/2023/understanding-iso27001-2022-people-process-technology.pdf

Tunggal, A. (2022, May 12). *What is an Information Security Policy?* Www.upguard.com.

https://www.upguard.com/blog/information-security-policy

Tunggal, A. T. (2023, October 24). *How to Perform a Cybersecurity Risk Assessment (2023 Guide) | UpGuard.* Www.upguard.com, https://www.upguard.com/blog/how-to-perform-a-cybersecurity-risk-assessment

12 Benefits of ISO 27001 Compliance and Certification - DataGuard. (n.d.). Www.dataguard.co.uk. https://www.dataguard.co.uk/blog/benefits-of-ISO27001

Unni, A. (2021, December 23). *4 Reasons Why Your Company Should Get ISO 27001 Compliant.* Www.stickmancyber.com. https://www.stickmancyber.com/cybersecurity-blog/4-reasons-why-your-company-should-get-ISO27001-compliant

V, A. (2023, December 12). *ISO 27001:2022 Project Plan: The Power of Strategic Project Planning.* ISO Templates and Documents Download. https://ISO.docs.com/blogs/ISO27001-isms/project-plan

What are the key features of an ISMS? | Answers. (n.d.). Www.6clicks.com. Retrieved December 15, 2023, from https://www.6clicks.com/resources/answers/what-are-the-key-features-of-an-isms

What is an Information Security Policy and What Should it Include? (2021, June 4). Securityscorecard.com. https://securityscorecard.com/blog/what-is-an-information-security-policy-and-what-should-it-include